The common sense guide to dealing
with life's ups and downs.

JUST
HELP
YOURSELF

TOM LUCAS

Just Help Yourself – The common sense guide to dealing with life's ups and downs

©Tom Lucas

ISBN: 978-1-906316-83-9

All rights reserved.

Published in 2011 by HotHive Books, Evesham, UK.

www.thehothive.com

The right of Tom Lucas to be identified as the author of this work has been asserted by him in accordance with the Copyright, Designs and Patents Act 1988.

A CIP record of this book is available from the British Library.

No part of this publication may be reproduced in any form or by any means without prior permission from the author.

Printed in the UK by TJ International, Padstow

This book is dedicated to all those who have needed some help along life's journey.
Enjoy the read, enjoy your life.

Contents

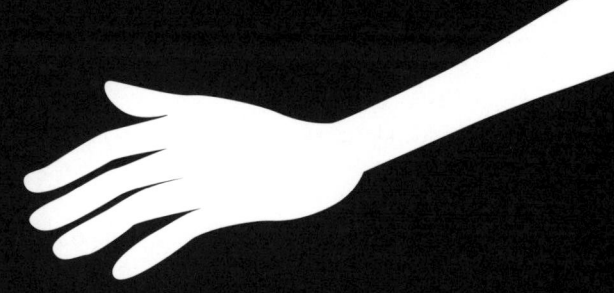

Acknowledgements

I would like to take this opportunity to publicly thank my wife, Bridie, for her sustaining patience and support.

To my daughters Collette and Roisin for keeping me in my place!

To my dear friends Gary and Eileen; Joe and Ellen, George and Ann-Maria; George and Mary Rose, for their valiant effort to keep my feet on terra firma!

To Bill Gaughan at 999 designs for a marvellous book cover (who said nothing good ever came out of Castlemilk!)

To Jim Spence at the BBC for his sense of humour.

To Terry Butcher for his kind words.

To Paul and Carroll at Sidekix.

To Raymond Boyle (artist) my therapist!

To Joe Logan at Loft Management and Norrie Innes at RockDM-C, whose help pushed the book over the line!

Finally to Christine McPherson without whose help and encouragement this book would not have been possible.

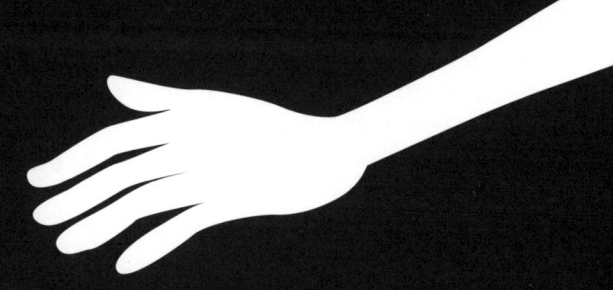

Foreword by Terry Butcher

The mind is so important in football – in fact, in sport generally. When I was manager at Motherwell Football Club, I felt the optimism and belief of our squad was wrong and that we needed help to work on that.

Tom Lucas had been working with other clubs and with individual players, and I felt he could help us. I arranged for him to come in before every game to talk to the boys before I did. My players were a bit dubious when he first arrived, but soon they began to focus more effectively on what they had to do.

I felt our biggest problem was a mental weakness. Our expectation levels weren't high, but one of the first things Tom did was to have a secret ballot, where he asked the players to write down where they thought we would finish in the SPL in the coming season. There were one or two who thought we would finish in the top two, and another couple who thought tenth and eleventh, but the majority thought mid-table. I felt it was a positive start, and so did they. It was a clever piece of psychology, but it sums Tom up.

He has a knack for breaking big problems down into smaller, manageable ones using a positive approach and, in many cases, basic common sense. As far as I'm concerned the mind is a wonderful thing, and I find it hard to believe that there are still some clubs who don't use psychologists. Even if it helps only one player it has to be useful for the team, and the odds are it will help more than one.

Tom picks things out from other sports, taking as examples people like American Tour de France champion Lance Armstrong who overcame cancer to become the world's greatest cyclist. He started to explain to my players about reaching the top of Everest by the end of the season and, as with every long walk, it begins with the first step. This book can show you how to reach your individual Everest, slowly but surely, overcoming pitfalls and problems along the way. I just wish I'd had someone to help me in this way earlier in my career.

Terry Butcher
Former captain of England and currently Manager of Inverness Caledonian Thistle

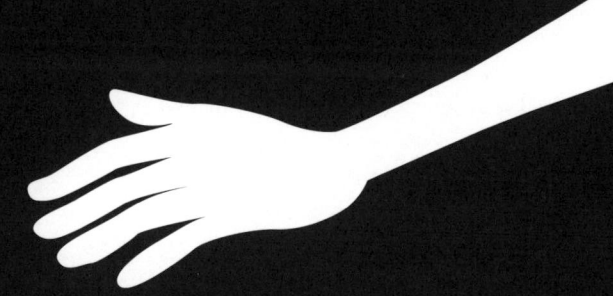

Introduction

The world is full of books on 'How to get rich quickly', 'How to win friends', 'How to succeed in business', 'How to succeed in relationships', 'How to...' etc.

So why read *this* book? How can I make a difference to your life? The simple answer is: I can't... but *you* can!

There are no guarantees with this book, no quick fixes, no easy options. So why would you want to read it? Because this book will challenge you to:

- look at ways to improve your life
- improve your self-confidence
- improve the way you navigate your way around life
- see yourself in a more positive light

More importantly, it can encourage you to deal with setbacks, disappointments, adversity and disasters and change how you deal with life in order to follow your dreams and reach that elusive pot of gold at the end of the rainbow called 'happiness'.

If you have the courage to read on and are prepared to face the challenges that life presents to you, then this book is perfect for you.

I want to help you to help yourself to a much fuller life with straightforward, easy-to-follow ideas and suggestions. There are no panaceas to changing your lifestyle, other than what you want to change.

At this stage all you have to answer is, are you ready to:

- take the first tentative steps to changing your perspective of yourself?
- begin to discover the 'real' you?
- challenge yourself to a new and improved quality of life?

If the answer is yes, then read on!

This book is based primarily on what I call CSP – Common Sense Psychology – basically a common sense approach to life, combined with a little bit of psychology, philosophy and anything else that might help you.

There is an old saying that if common sense is so common, how come so many people don't seem either to have it, or to use it? We do all have some common sense, but we don't use it enough. Instead we look for the 'hidden' meaning, complications and over-solutions to problems/issues, yet most of the time this is futile and a waste of energy. There are many occasions when we make situations more complex than they need to be. The answer is, as often as not, quite literally staring us in the face: OURSELVES!

CSP is all about you and what you do with your life; how you interact with others. CSP does not offer any instant remedies in dealing with problems. But, by sticking to the principles I outline, you will immediately increase the chances of achieving your full potential.

You will learn to realise that you are a valued human being, and that you are accepted and loved for who and what you are. If you don't think highly of yourself, how can you expect others to think highly of you?

This book will challenge you to become more confident, more self-assured, have greater self-esteem and, eventually, more control over your life. CSP is not a recent phenomenon. As the saying goes, 'there is nothing new under the sun'. But just sometimes we get an eclipse. CSP is a bit like an eclipse. Its roots lie in the belief that by approaching life with a little bit of CSP, we can navigate our way with as little damage as possible to ourselves and, hopefully, reach our destination of self-fulfillment.

CSP recognises that not everyone can be a great artist, musician, writer or sportsperson, but we can all aim to make the most of our lives and be all that we can be. I may not be able to run a mile in under four minutes, but I can run a mile! I may not be able to write a best-selling book, but I can write a book. Whatever it is that you want to aspire to, you have to believe that you can do it. CSP will help you to understand yourself, allow you to grow rich in experience, help you to come to terms with who you are and guide you to become who you want to be. By taking the CSP approach to life, you will be able to face those tough decisions we all have to make in a self-assured manner and with more self-confidence and greater self-belief.

I have to be honest here, this book will ask you to take a risk. That risk is discovering who you really are – and what you could become. It will not turn you into something you can't be, but it will open your life to the endless possibilities which await you when you release yourself from the mental straitjacket that currently enfolds you.

We are all faced with choices and decisions that affect our lives. Unfortunately too many of us neglect to take the decisions that involve our dreams and desires. Instead, they get lost as we settle down into the routine of work, family and commitments. Somewhere along the way we stop developing ourselves. The net result is that some of us have become disenchanted, unfulfilled, disappointed and dissatisfied with life. In the current uncertain times, it is even more important that you look after your own wellbeing – physically, mentally and spiritually.

Often we are guilty of thinking and worrying too much. Over-thinking can lead to inaction, stagnation and uncertainty. There is a time and a place for thinking and a time and a place for doing! The time for doing is *now*!

You can wait too long for things to be in the right place, the right order and the right time. If you wait for the stars and the planets to be in alignment and the right conditions to be in place before you start to make a change, you'll be waiting forever! Waiting for the 'right' conditions is an easy way of mentally conditioning yourself never to make a start. All that happens is you get stuck in a comfort zone of inactivity and excuses and you condemn yourself to a life of 'If only' and 'Maybe'.

There is no magic formula to bring about change in your life. But CSP will enable you to make sense of your world and invite you to explore the 'real' you.

- There are no short-cuts to changes in your lifestyle.
- There are no quick fixes that will give you everything you are looking for to improve your current situation.
- There are no remedies that will give you the answers to all your doubts, anxieties, fears, hopes and desires.

Throughout this book I will, however, provide you with ideas and suggestions to select from, experiment with, reject outright or use, to find something that appeals to you. In other words, you become your own social scientist!

It is precisely because we are all different that there is no one-stop, fix-all solution for everybody. Instead you have to look around, select, then experiment with different ideas and options that suit you and that you are comfortable with. Always remember: nobody thinks like you, nobody feels like you, nobody laughs like you, or talks like you. You are unique! You are a unique individual and, as such, You know what You need better than anyone else.

Each chapter will help you to face up to the daily challenges of life using analogies from sport and everyday life. By using a CSP approach to situations, you may find that you feel as if you already know the answer – and you probably do! It is just that you have not thought things through in a simple manner. Now you can take the first tentative steps to changing the negative view you have of yourself and make a fresh, positive start.

Yesterday is gone, tomorrow is still to come, today is all the time you have. Don't throw it away! By looking after 'Your Self' you will become mentally stronger. You will enrich your life and the lives of those around you. Your personal growth and development will increase and you will be more content within yourself. You have nothing to lose and a lot to gain. These changes are for life.

The only guarantee I can give you is that everything changes – nothing remains static. You have a real choice to make – either decide to embrace change, or have change thrust upon you. You can influence the first or surrender to the second.

So, the crucial question is:

Are you ready to challenge YOUR SELF to be the person you have always wanted to be? Then, let's go!

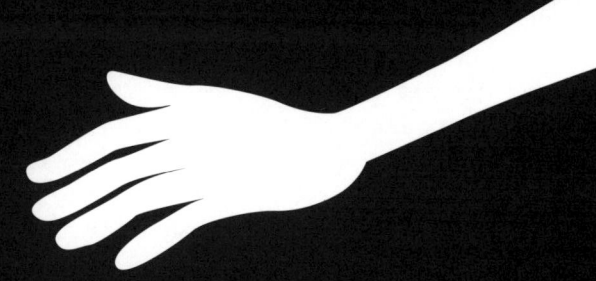

Chapter One

'Just Help Your Self To...'

Most of us are pretty familiar with the phrase 'Just help yourself…'. It's usually heard at social functions or parties, and invariably refers to food and drink. But nobody has ever asked us to help ourselves to happiness, peace or good health – those are things we have to find for ourselves.

Helping yourself to happiness is a relatively simple concept. First you need to identify what it is that is making you unhappy, and then change it. Simple? Of course life is not as simple as that, and to make any change in your lifestyle may be more of a problem than you care to tackle. Yet by simply shifting your focus to looking at what is 'good' in your life, you immediately find that helping yourself to some happiness is not so hard after all.

Each day, every day is a brand new opportunity to challenge yourself to be happy. By the time you get to the bus stop, train station or into your car, there are at least 10–20 things to brighten your day! Tomorrow morning when you wake up, just stop to think about the day ahead and what you want to get out of it. Look at the flowers, the sky, the colours of the day, listen to the sound of birds, feel the wind on your face! There is so much to be happy about.

If you're out of a job, living in a depressed area, surrounded by poverty or in a broken relationship, you probably don't feel like being 'happy'. But you can help yourself. Whatever situation you are in, you can change your focus. It may be that your self-help to happiness is to be found in helping others to find their happiness. Don't allow yourself to wallow in self-pity. Go out and help others and you will be helping yourself to your own happiness and peace.

Being unhappy is a state of mind, so you can change that state of mind to being a bit less unhappy and a bit happier. You don't need to be unhappy – just change those negative thoughts that are making you unhappy. Think of it a bit like changing channels on the TV, and change your negative thoughts immediately into positive ones.

Helping yourself to a new life requires you to start thinking differently. Once you start to think more positively, you will be amazed at what changes you can bring to your current situation. A positive approach to everyday life will ultimately pay dividends for you. But it is not a one-day wonder. To change your approach to life and help yourself to a better lifestyle requires you to have determination, commitment and staying power to make those changes work.

- Nobody can make you unhappy – unless you let them.
- Being happy or unhappy is often a state of mind.
- Take control of your life by starting today to 'Just help yourself to…'

Many people think that they can find happiness by seeing other people happy – but that's not always the case. Finding so-called happiness in other people's joy is short-sighted and not really meaningful. It is a false type of happiness. We can only find 'true' happiness and fulfilment when we reach a state of mind where we accept ourselves for who we are, and not who we think we want to be. Inner happiness is felt within our own being. So we should stop looking for happiness in other people's lives.

Certainly we can share in their good fortune, but we can't live it with them or truly experience it. You have to go out and help yourself to your own happiness. Nobody will come knocking on your door and invite you to make changes.

Helping yourself to anything requires motivation and a commitment from you. But it's amazing how much you can achieve in your life when you just let yourself go and free yourself from the chains of boredom and mediocrity. Nobody can live your life for you. You have to help yourself to live your life as fully as possible. So why not help yourself to the good things? It may be that you don't know what they are – or maybe you think they are unattainable. First, what is your perception of the good things in life? Is it peace, friendship, material goods, money, financial security, being free from stress and anxiety?

Helping yourself to anything requires you to motivate yourself! Nobody can motivate for you. You can be inspired by people, a book, a film, a play or whatever, but the ultimate motivator is YOU. The motivation has to come from within – somewhere deep inside your psyche there has to be a *motivation* to make a change – a change to your life.

CASE STUDY

I was 18 years of age and living in Easterhouse, Glasgow – one of the worst housing estates in the UK. I had been a failure at school and for three years in a row had failed my O Levels (now Standard Grades), so was forced to leave school with no qualifications. I had suffered for years with chronic asthma, which had caused me to miss a lot of school – and childhood – and led to some nasty bullying. By that stage, I was in a dead-end job, going nowhere.

One sunny Saturday morning I was leaning out of my bedroom window. I could see most of the east end of the city spread out before me. I was scanning the streets and houses, and feeling quite depressed about my situation. I desperately wanted to get out of the drudgery, poverty and violence that were endemic in the housing scheme, and I wanted to escape the systematic bullying. What could I do to change things around?

I made two decisions that fundamentally altered my life. The first was to join Shettleston Harriers Athletics Club. I had always been interested in athletics but could not participate because of my health. But by joining the Harriers, I started on the path to improving my general health and eventually curing myself of asthma.

My second decision was to enrol in evening classes at Langside Further Education College, to try to do something about my lack of educational qualifications. Over the next two years, I managed to gain several O Levels and Highers, which then led me to realise a lifelong dream to go to university.

The hopelessness of my situation was my motivation – but by taking action, I ensured that my situation was no longer hopeless!

V/hy not start today with a simple first step? Say to yourself: 'Today I am going to help myself to…' If you say that to yourself over and over again, the chances are that you will not only start to believe it but will also start to act on it. You could help yourself to start to learn new skills, find a new job, a new relationship, or whatever you want to do.

Help yourself to thoughts about being more positive and you will start to think about the things you can do and achieve, rather than what you previously thought you couldn't do. Success or failure begins and ends in the mind. Your mind and thoughts can tell you to stop thinking negatively and start thinking positively, but it is a constant daily battle in which you have to overcome the dark forces of negativity and doubt.

By helping yourself, you can of course help others. That is the spin-off when you begin to help yourself. Others will feel good for you and will treat you differently, so there is a knock-on effect when you start to change. It's called the DOMINO effect, i.e. when you start to change, other things will start to change.

There is a chain reaction. Helping yourself to anything in life involves a risk, but there is an old saying: 'small risk = small change; big risk = big change'.

There is always a risk that you might not be as successful in making changes as you would have hoped for, but there is also the risk that you will change and that that change will be forever. One thing is for sure: nothing will happen unless you take that risk.

Stagnation in your personal life and personal development is the only thing you can guarantee if you do nothing. An unfulfilled life awaits you. A life full of regrets of 'ifs, buts, maybes and could-have-beens' is staring at you right now. That is the price you will pay for not following your dreams, fulfilling your talents or realising your ambitions.

Not everyone can be a great painter, musician, athlete, entrepreneur or inventor. We can, however, all improve our lives by living them to the full and enjoying the journey through life. You can help yourself to a healthier lifestyle, to a new job, to writing that book, to a new career, to a new exercise regime, even to a new hairstyle! Give your creative talents a chance to flourish.

Taking the first step is always the hardest. Think of it like a baby trying to take those first steps on his own after weeks of wandering around holding on to the furniture. He knows the route he wants to take to reach that interesting-looking object on the other side of the room. By taking those first few unaided steps he might fall over – maybe a few times – but he will pick himself up and try again until eventually he can stay on his feet, take a few steps, then a few more and eventually reach his target. And look at the delight on his face when he gets there. That could be you!

Courage and a sense of self-belief are required to take that first step on the ladder of change. The courage you require is with you right now – and there are plenty of people who will support you. Making that change to your lifestyle requires mental courage. If you think you can do it – you will! Believe that change is possible and it is. Helping yourself to a lifestyle change is a lifetime commitment to keep on challenging yourself to realise those ambitions and dreams. Just remember that there are very few individuals who are 'overnight' successes. Most have taken years to achieve their goals.

CASE STUDY

A young professional footballer came to see me regarding his future. He had just been 'released' from his current club but desperately wanted to continue as a professional footballer. He had an opportunity to go on trial at another club but was feeling anxious and nervous about his prospects, because his confidence and self-esteem had taken a severe knock. He was afraid that his career would be over.

After several long discussions, we devised a plan that would enable him to face the future with a greater degree of confidence. The plan consisted of:

- improving his technical ability
- improving his overall fitness level
- implementing a dietary programme
- introducing a sports psychology programme
- reviewing his current lifestyle
- increasing his commitment and dedication
- establishing realistic goals for 1–3 years

Having agreed to the whole package, the footballer began to take more control over his life ... and it paid off. He went on to play over 200 games for his new club and became not only captain of that club, but also captained his country – something he had never even dreamt could happen!

Many people give up too soon because the going is too tough or because they cannot handle setbacks or disappointments. This need not apply to you. If you feel that there is something missing, that something has not been achieved in your life, or there is a dream that is unfulfilled – then help yourself to start to achieve. Who is to say you cannot do it? Who is to say it is impossible for you? Who is to say you cannot make those changes to your life? The only person who can stop you is YOU!

Realising your dreams or not, largely depends on YOU. The quality of your life will depend on how much YOU are prepared to put into it. Don't sell yourself short by just accepting things as they are, or as you think they will always be. Reach out and explore what possibilities are open to you.

The current climate may not seem like the right time to contemplate making changes to your lifestyle, but you couldn't be more wrong. The only right time to make a change is now! There is no point in waiting for the right 'conditions' or for some inter-planetary alignment. There will never be 'ideal' circumstances that will allow you to make the right decision at the right time. When you do decide to make a change, be prepared to find that your outlook on life will also change. Things that troubled you in the past or made you angry may not seem so troublesome after you have made some changes.

Start by getting yourself into a positive frame of mind. Work on turning those negative thoughts into positive thoughts. As soon as a negative thought comes into your head, quickly switch that channel to something positive. Practise doing this until you are in control of your thoughts. Don't let negative thoughts take a hold over you. You know they don't do you any good – so why have them? Why allow the misery of feeling negative to overtake and control your life?

Being positive requires a lot of hard work. Look on it as a drive down the motorway at 70 mph. If you are on the motorway heading for the destination called Negativity, pull over at the next exit and, when you have safely stopped, re-set your sat-nav for the destination called Positive. Once you have done that, you are clear to re-start your journey.

Your journey will have many twists and turns, but if you are clear and determined about where you want to get to, you will eventually arrive there safely.

The key to life is to:

- be flexible
- be determined
- be positive
- be confident in yourself
- look for opportunities for personal growth
- help yourself

The next time you are at a function or social gathering and the buffet is announced with 'Just help yourself…' remember to help yourself to some happiness at the same time!

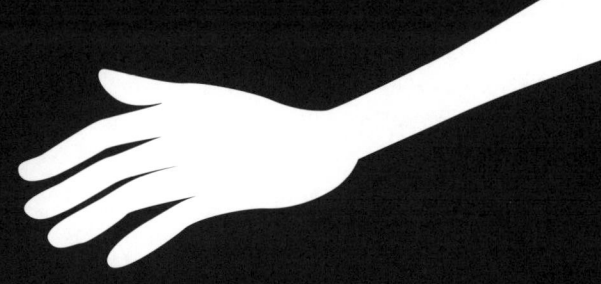

Chapter Two

Who R U?

In the cult American TV series, *CSI*, the theme tune – sung by The Who – is entitled, 'Who Are You?'. The series itself is all about trying to identify people who have been murdered or have gone missing.

Do you really know who you are? All of us at some time – perhaps subconsciously – have posed the question, 'Who am I?' By asking who we are, we are trying to be aware of our 'self' – and this Reflective Self is vitally important to us. Once we become fully aware of who we are, we can accept ourselves as a valued human being in our own right, someone with a contribution to make.

Our self-esteem and our identity are important to us. They define us. They provide us with a 'reference point' both historically and anthropologically. We all have the need to 'belong' to a particular group, community, tribe, clan or family. By belonging we find strength, a bond that enables us to identify who we truly are.

The recent rush by people to find their ancestors and trace their family history, and the popularity of the BBC series, *Who Do You Think You Are?*, clearly highlights our need to establish who we are and where we have come from.

By being self-aware and identifying who you are, you can take confidence in the knowledge that you do belong.

Being self-aware is crucial in every aspect of your life. Without proper self-awareness you are limited and unfulfilled in what you do and who you are. You are stuck in a time-frame and cannot move. Your life is incomplete until you recognise and embrace who you are. Being self-aware and aware of yourself will allow you to develop and grow.

The next time you look in the bathroom mirror, ask yourself this question: 'Who do I see?' Once you have answered, remember that the biggest obstacle to your self-esteem is staring right back at you – YOU! If you can overcome YOU on a daily basis, then you have a chance of maintaining a high level of self-awareness and self-esteem.

I always spend some time in the morning looking at myself in the mirror. I'd say it was to remind myself how good-looking I am, but that would be hotly disputed by my two daughters! Being aware of who you are is vital to your self-belief and inner-confidence.

- Who you are defines you and places you in the world.
- Who you are gives you an anchor to determine your footprint and where you are in the planet.

By being more aware of yourself, you can start doing some of the things that you have always wanted to do. Self-awareness involves finding out what makes you want to do something and having the determination, confidence and commitment to go and do it. Self-awareness is being realistic, but hopeful, in relation to your expectations.

Here's an example. When I started running to try to improve my health, I found that it did help my chronic asthma. But no matter how hard I trained, I could not break the four-minute-mile barrier. I realised and accepted that I did not have the talent or ability to do it, but I became healthier and able to control my asthma. Sure, it would have been nice to have run a mile in under four minutes, but I achieved other benefits instead.

Being aware of your self will give you the confidence to deal with life's ups and downs. It is not easy to deal with setbacks and disappointments, but by having a greater self-awareness you can draw strength from them and find the determination to continue.

Undoubtedly there are some setbacks in life which are harder to deal with than others. They can make us feel worthless and inadequate, despair at what has happened and feel that the whole world is against us. There is no easy answer to that feeling. But by persevering in the knowledge of your own value as a human being – totally convinced that you are worthy and that you can influence change – you will gather the willpower to keep going.

None of us likes to feel inadequate or worthless. We all want to be liked and feel needed, but there is no point in feeling sorry for yourself. If you really know yourself, you will accept that these feelings are only temporary. Your self-awareness will give you the courage and determination to get up and start again.

Rejection in any shape or form is hard to take. Many of us have received rejection letters for jobs that we applied for. Many of us have experienced 'emotional' rejection. Your Inner Self will help you cope with those situations and help you to find a solution.

One way of helping yourself is to analyse what you say to yourself. Don't worry, everybody talks to themselves. We do it subconsciously. Every time we have a thought, we are actually talking to ourselves. Whether we do it vocally or in the silence of our minds – we all do it. But how we talk to ourselves is important to how we rationalise and make sense of our world.

Sometimes we can talk ourselves into being negative and seeing everything in a poor light, and this makes things a lot worse than they really are. We can convince ourselves that there is nothing we can do and we should accept the situation we are in as fate. If that is how you feel, isn't it about time you stopped thinking this way? What a waste of mental energy! Instead, start to 'talk' things around.

- Remind yourself of all the good things in your life – and don't say that you don't have any – you do!
- Talk to yourself about what you want to happen, instead of what you don't want to happen.
- Keep reminding yourself of your worth.
- Be aware that you *do* have a lot to offer.
- Keep speaking to yourself in a positive manner – talk yourself *up* and not down.
- Remind yourself of happier times, when you were successful, when you felt good about what you achieved. It might be something like when you passed your driving test, gained a promotion, learned to swim or ride a bike, or passed an exam. Whatever it was, remind yourself of what that feeling felt like and that you did it – and that you can do it again!

The world is full of negative people who will want to keep you down. Usually these people are failures themselves, they don't want you to succeed so they keep telling you that you can't do this or achieve that.

You have the power to reject their negative views, but you must remain strong and resolute in the face of their negativity. Knowing who and what you really are will depend on your view of yourself. You can either accept other people's view of you, or you can reject it; the choice is yours. Be comfortable with who you are.

In this fast-paced 24/7 world, we are bombarded with adverts extolling the virtues of this or that product which will make us feel younger, enhance our shape, or look more attractive. They don't work!

Sure, they can disguise or alter how you look, but they cannot alter who you are! All the products and makeovers in the world cannot alter your real personality.

- YOU are who YOU are.
- You are a valued human being with a lot to offer.
- You have skills and talents that nobody else has – you are unique.
- There is nobody quite like you in the world.
- Be aware of yourself and your Self will be aware of you.

Take some time out to reflect on who you are, and spend a few moments to examine where you want to go and how you are going to get there. Think of something you really want to do or achieve, and something you want to change about yourself. Then set yourself some goals for today, tomorrow and the future. Goal-setting is a valuable way of giving yourself direction in life. Start by setting some small daily goals, and soon you will find that the change you were looking for has already begun to happen. Just how much do you want to change? And what are you prepared to do about it?

It is said that we are the products of our own history and backgrounds, that we are programmed to act in a certain way, pre-conditioned to respond in a particular manner. However, we all have the ability to shape our own history and create our own background. No sociologists, psychologists or philosophers say that you have to accept things as they are.

How many people do you know who have 'broken' the stereotypical mould that society has created for them? How many people have set out to explore and challenge themselves, to find out what they can achieve?

CASE STUDY

A 19-year-old amateur golfer was in the process of turning professional. This was a big decision for him, bearing in mind that very few golfers actually make it in the world of professional golf. After a series of meetings and discussions, a 'goal-setting' plan was produced that would cover the next 3–5 years.

But before embarking on this exercise, it was explained that certain aspects of goal-setting have to be kept in mind. The criteria were that the goals must be:

- achievable
- believable
- controllable
- measurable
- desirable
- compatible

The golfer was asked to think about what he would like to achieve and where he 'saw' himself in that time. He set a target for himself for the next five years, by which time he would be 24 years of age. With his long-term goal identified, the next part of goal-setting was to produce some intermediate goals to help him along the way, which would maintain his motivation and give him direction. These intermediate goals were for 1–3 years ahead.

But even these goals could seem far away. Perhaps the most important aspect of goal-setting is the introduction of short-term or daily goals. These make the whole process of goal-setting much more effective. If the amateur golfer wants to be a professional golfer, what is he/she going to do about it in the next five minutes; hour; day; week; month; year?

Setting specific daily goals and pursuing them in a systematic way separates those who want to meet the challenges and want to excel from those who actually do. Once you have decided that something is worth pursuing, you can apply goal-setting in virtually every area of your life. Whether you want to enjoy success in sport, business or write a book, the basic procedure is the same. It is only your commitment and specific goals that are different. Remember the meter of life is running. So don't run out of time – start now!

Not everyone has the genetic make-up or courage to leave their community, society or country to discover new shores. Your circumstances may mean that is impossible for you to up sticks and make a new, fresh start. But, even within your current lifestyle and situation, you can make small yet significant changes which can hugely affect your life.

In the great scheme of things we are all 'Jekyll and Hyde'. We use our personalities to suit the occasion we find ourselves in. For instance, we are not the same person at work as we are at home or with friends. Who you are will depend on which stage you are appearing. It will depend on whether it is a matinee performance, a first night or a dress rehearsal. Who you are is the central question of your being – who you want to be will depend on how you act out your dreams and aspirations.

So, if our lives are just an 'act' then why not decide to act differently? Your life is not a dress rehearsal – you only have one shot at it! Being aware of your Self and who you are will help to define you and enable you to make your way in the world.

Being at one with yourself will give you comfort, confidence and inner-peace. Everybody is searching for who they are. Some will spend a fortune searching out their history and background. Most of us do not have the luxury or time to investigate our ancestral heritage, but we still have a perspective on who we are by the family history that has been handed down to us. Our names are precious to us – they define us – they identify who we are.

- Be aware of your Self and who you are.
- Take your place in the world.
- Make a statement of who you are and what you want to be.
- Don't let anybody put you down or put you off.

- Be proud of who you are.
- Remind yourself of how unique you are.
- Be confident within yourself.
- Search for new horizons – stretch yourself.
- Be all that you can be – be YOU!
- Don't let anyone steal your dreams.
- Be aware of your Self and tap into your potential gold mine.

WHO are you?

You are YOU!

You'll be amazed at what you can achieve if you put your mind to it.

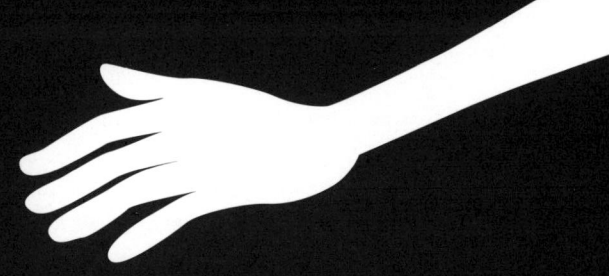

Chapter Three

Don't Hide Your Self Away

Too many of us hide our true selves away from other people and situations. Sometimes we're afraid that if we put ourselves forward or make a suggestion, we will be looked upon as arrogant, pushy or conceited. But by not offering our ideas, opinions or suggestions, we can be looked upon as withdrawn, shy and introverted.

It is not easy to be confident in public. Do you:

- tend to just fade away in the background, afraid to make a fool of yourself?
- sit back and let other people hog the limelight?
- prefer not to be the centre of attention?

Our introspection and timidity can cause us enormous mental pain, but unfortunately we are the victims of our own cultural upbringing. We are not encouraged to display our talents or skills, because that is often seen as a sign of arrogance and conceitedness. So the net result over the years is a tendency to shy away from appearing to show off.

This condition is still prevalent in our society and, sadly, it begins in the home and continues in the classroom. By the time we have left school, our self-confidence, self-esteem, self-awareness and self-belief are non-existent.

Unfortunately, by being like this we miss out on many potential opportunities for personal growth and development. But all is not lost. This condition is a state of mind and can be turned around. All we have to do is improve the skills which will allow us to perform comfortably in any social setting. This can be achieved by 'ACTING' confidently.

- First, you THINK better about yourself.
- Then REHEARSE the part you want to play.
- Finally, you ACT the part for real.

If you are lacking in self-confidence, by 'acting' confidently you can become confident. Always remember that in any social gathering, conference or public meeting, everybody is 'acting'. Some people are better at it than others, but all of them will be acting. They will be acting out their part according to their personality.

As we've discussed before, we are all 'Jekyll and Hyde' characters. We know that we act differently when we are at home, at work or socially. We can feel threatened and insecure when we are away from the comfort and security of our own home and surroundings. We can also feel anxious and stressed, and that can lead us to be seen as withdrawn, shy, introverted or even boring.

John Grisham

- got up at 5am to write his first novel *A Time to Kill*

- approached 26 publishers – sold less than 1000 copies

- took responsibility to promote himself at weekends

- there are now over 10 million copies of his books in print

By being more self-confident and more self-assured, you can create enough of an impression to allow yourself to pass off an event without too much stress and anxiety. You can overcome your feelings of inadequacy and lack of confidence simply by pretending to be outgoing.

Try this – even for a little while – at the next function or event you are at. Start by going up to a complete stranger and introducing yourself. Remember there will be a lot of people feeling the way you do, and that might include the person you introduce yourself to.

Practise doing this at home before you set off. All you have to do is follow these steps:

- Step 1: Identify someone who appears to be on their own.
- Step 2: Watch him/her closely for a few minutes.
- Step 3: Mentally rehearse your introduction, 'Hello, I am…'
- Step 4: Offer to shake hands – look into their eyes.
- Step 5: Ask them to introduce themselves.
- Step 6: Engage in conversation (rehearse some questions).

Simple? Yes, it is! It's not rocket science. The key is to keep practising because 'Practice makes *permanent*'! Practice doesn't make perfect – because there is no such thing as perfection. But if we practise something long enough, the skill will become *permanent*! Once we learn something, we can't unlearn it – it's like riding a bike, learning to swim, or driving a car.

1. Practise in front of a mirror.
2. Rehearse what you want to say.

3. Believe that you can do it.

4. Mentally go over it.

5. Act as if you are going onto a stage.

Go on, surprise yourself! The world is full of people who have the flair, talent or skill to be a writer, sportsperson, musician or teacher, but somehow they have not managed to bring it to the fore.

Albert Einstein

- did not speak until the age of 4

- could not read until he was 7

- was described by one teacher as 'Mentally slow, unsociable and adrift forever in his foolish dreams'

- was expelled from one college and refused entry to another

Far too many of us hide our talents away because if we do attempt to show them, there is always somebody who will try to put us down with a negative comment like 'you will never be able to do…'. They will constantly tell you that you are not good enough, strong enough, tall enough, etc. These kinds of comments are all too common in our 'negative' society.

We know that not everyone can be a great writer, musician or athlete, but every one of us has talents or skills, and we can achieve a lot more if we are given the right type of encouragement. It is never too late to try.

Why not start right now and write the first sentence of that book you have always wanted to write? Stop reading now and go and write that first sentence. Done that? Good, now write the second and the third and so on. How about the poem you have always wanted to write, or the painting or sculpture you've wanted to create? Sign up for a local art or music class and take that first step!

As you explore your talents/skills to the full, your self-confidence will grow. The enjoyment in achieving something is a treasure to behold and it is something that nobody can take away from you. We inhibit ourselves by having too many negative thoughts which prevent us from getting more out of life than we currently do.

Whatever talents, skills or interests you have, you owe it to your Self to use them to the fullest, to continually work on them and to let them flourish. The adrenaline rush you get when you start using your talents is amazing. And the idea is to build on that initial adrenaline and watch yourself develop as a person in the process.

Colonel Sanders

- worked for 40 years as a railroad labourer

- visited nearly 500 restaurants in an attempt to sell his Kentucky Fried Chicken recipe

- was aged 65 when he finally succeeded

You are a valued human being with something to offer. Step into the bright new day and the bright new You. Be happy with who you are and what you can be. Inside of you there is a person with untapped skills/talents screaming to get out. How long has it been since you used your skills/talents? Are they lying dormant? Have you let your personal development wither on the vine?

You owe it to yourself to shake off the manacles of doubt that have shackled you for too long. Stop listening to those voices of negativity that are in your head. Change them into something positive. Every time a negative thought comes into your head, just snap your fingers and think of something positive. It doesn't really matter if you never become a famous writer, artist, musician, etc. What it boils down to is how you maximise your talents and skills and take them as far as they can develop.

It's not the destination but the journey we undertake that is the issue. The journey of self-development is what is at stake. If you hide yourself away, you lose the opportunity to find out just how good you can be. You also lose the opportunity to grow, and in later years you may come to regret those moments or, even worse, look back on a life not fulfilled.

Thomas Edison

- made 10,000 attempts before successfully inventing the electric light

- was asked what it was like to fail so many times. He replied: 'I did not fail, I simply discovered thousands of ways that wouldn't produce light.'

Now is the time for you to come out into the open and be your self! It's time now for you to take control of your life and take control of your aspirations and dreams.

- Don't spend your life being envious of other people and their success, achievements, skills or talents.
- Nurture your own talents and skills. Don't let anyone tell you that you can't do this or achieve that.
- Write that first sentence in your book, pick up the telephone directory and make an appointment to learn how to drive, go along to the local art class, or join that gym. They are all waiting for you. Take the first step – now!
- Find an art class, pottery class, flower arranging class, dance class, tai chi class, yoga class, swimming class – whatever it is that you have always wanted to do – do it now! You know you want to.
- Switch off your TV – get off the couch and go and discover YOUR SELF!

Taking the first step is always the hardest. After that it becomes easier. Remember the old saying: 'Yard by yard it's too hard; inch by inch it's a cinch.' You will look back in later years at the difference that first step made to your life.

Too many people give up on things because they fall into the trap of throwing themselves into something – like keeping fit – only to find that they have done too much too quickly. So they drop out. The result is that they fail to keep it going.

Wilma Rudolph

- was 20th of 22 children

- born prematurely, her survival was doubtful

- when she was 4, she contracted scarlet fever

- she was left with a paralysed leg

- at the age of 9 she removed the metal brace on her leg

- by 13 she had developed a rhythmic walk, which doctors said was a miracle

- at 13 she decided to be a runner

- she entered a race and came in last

- for the next two years, every race she entered she finished last

- one day she won a race... then another

This little girl, who was told she would never walk again, went on to win three Olympic Gold Medals!

Instead of starting gently and moving along at a comfortable pace, too many people give up because they have thrown themselves at something only to discover the one ingredient that is missing – ENJOYMENT.

- Don't forget to enjoy whatever it is you want to do.
- Take time, pride and pleasure in whatever activity you undertake.
- Don't be influenced by what other people say or do. They have their own life/agenda.
- Remember you are not in a race. You are doing this for your own self-fulfillment and pleasure.
- What you get out of something is equal to the amount of time, energy, commitment and patience you are prepared to put into it.

You don't want to end up as one of those people who have a lifetime of regrets and who protest 'If only I...' or 'I always wanted to...', 'I could have been ...'. There is a new world out there waiting for you. Why don't you go and get some of it?

Start by putting your TV off for one minute a day! Just sit back, relax and close your eyes. Let the sound of peace and quiet enter your mind. Think about what you could do in that one minute just for yourself. If you haven't read a book for a while – why don't you read one page? Start something and soon that minute without TV will become two, three, four, five minutes!

Eventually you will feel that you are doing something more creative with your life but, more importantly, you will actually be taking control of your life! You will control the TV remote, rather than the TV remote control you. You will have taken your life back and cut the umbilical television cord.

You will be able to step outside your present situation and embrace every day as a challenge. A challenge to change yourself; to stop hiding yourself away; a challenge to change your lifestyle. Do it today... not tomorrow, or the next day, or next week, or next month. Don't wait until the 'perfect' conditions are in place – they never will be. Don't wait until you think the time is right – or you will wait forever.

Act today! Act NOW!

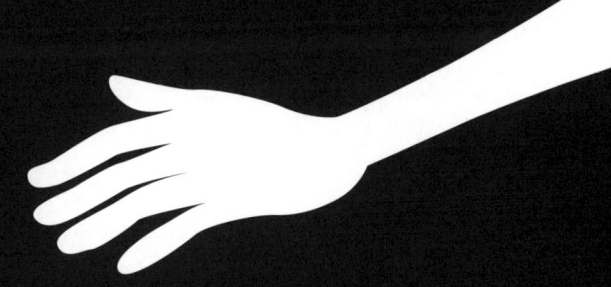

Chapter Four

Shop For Your Self

When you pop into your local supermarket, you don't stop to think about all the time psychologists and marketing people have spent working on product placement, promotions, design and strategic lay-out of the products.

Their job is to understand what makes you and I want to buy certain items and to anticipate our behavioural patterns, so they can strategically place items at just the right position to catch our eyes.

They even replicate smells that we associate with certain feelings and thoughts, in a bid to attract our attention and encourage us to purchase. How often has the aroma of freshly-baked bread, which might even have been 'imported' into the store, led you to the bakery department to buy something that wasn't on your list?

All manner of psychological 'tricks' and skills are deployed on a daily basis to influence shoppers and capture their attention.

The five key shelves listed below represent some of the main items you will find in most supermarkets. These shelves give a variety of items to choose from, but the final choice is ultimately ours.

CEREAL/OATS/SNACKS

INGREDIENTS

FRUIT/VEGETABLES

MILK/WATER/JUICE

BREAD/PASTA/MEAT/POTATOES

We are all well aware of the need to maintain a balanced diet for a healthy life, and most of us will use many of the products on these five shelves regularly. However, it is also important that we have a psychologically balanced life, otherwise we may make the wrong decisions or become ill.

I want to show you how the choices we make in the supermarket actually relate closely to the choices we need to make in our lives.

Cereal/oats/snacks

For many people, breakfast consists of cereal or porridge, fruit juice and toast. Having a good breakfast is the kick-start to their day. How do you start yours?

Most cereals contain a number of ingredients: from fibre to carbohydrates. But as much as your body needs a good start to the day in terms of food and nourishment, your mind also needs some 'mental food'. So as you munch on your toast, why don't you mentally prepare for the day ahead? Think of the meetings you may have to attend, the list of things you have to do, the people you have to face. No matter what job we are in – or maybe we are even searching for a job – we can all mentally prepare for the day ahead and put ourselves in a positive frame of mind.

It may be that there is something pressing which you have been putting off, or delaying. By mentally preparing and rehearsing over breakfast, we can give ourselves the confidence to tackle our tasks. How we think about the day ahead is manifested by what kind of frame of mind we are in. So breakfast is an ideal opportunity to take a few moments to set yourself some 'goals' for the day ahead or to make a 'to-do list' to help you focus and improve your mental wellbeing.

Just as a good healthy breakfast will give you some protection against viruses and illness, so a good mental breakfast will protect you against stress and anxiety. But make sure you also take appropriate breaks in the morning, lunchtime and in the afternoon. Taking time out helps to recharge your physical and mental batteries, so you must not neglect this important aspect of your SELF!

Ingredients

Ingredients are used in whatever meal we are going to cook. We know what ingredients are contained in any food, by studying the label and reading the amount of salt, carbohydrates, proteins, minerals, etc. So it is important that we read the labels carefully.

By the same token we need to carefully read the labels that affect our lives. What does your Label of Life say about you? What ingredients of life are needed or missing from your life? Do you have too much of one ingredient as opposed to another?

If you have too much ingredient called 'work', how does that impact on the rest of your life? Does your Label of Life carry a health warning? Take some time to study your life's ingredients and find out if you are leading a balanced lifestyle.

With food, health experts often warn that the contents may contain 'artificial flavouring/colouring' which can have side-effects. Does your life contain some 'artificial' issues that prevent you from leading a balanced and fruitful life? Maybe it's time for you to read your life label again and change the balance of your ingredients!

Fruit/vegetables

We all recognise the importance of eating enough fruit and vegetables, even if we don't actually manage the recommended five-a-day. In the Supermarket of Life some products are pre-packaged, some are free range. The choice is yours.

And so is the choice of the kind of lifestyle you want to have:

- You do not have to be a couch potato.
- You do not have to be overweight.
- You do not have to be unfit.
- You can do something about it.

Start by doing a little every day. Go for a five-minute walk, or stroll down to your local shop instead of taking the car.

There is no point in trying to do 30 minutes of exercise three times a week – as recommended by many medical/fitness professionals – if it has been a while since you have done any exercise at all. Instead, start gently and slowly and you are much more likely to keep going, gradually increasing your time, than if you are trying hard to maintain three 30/45 minute sessions. Starting slowly allows you to add to your time whenever you feel comfortable and confident that you can maintain the increase. And it's the same with eating fruit and vegetables.

We are advised to eat five pieces of fruit a day, but how many of us actually do? If you are out of the habit of eating fruit and veg, then it's extremely difficult to eat five pieces a day every day. Instead start with one a day and then gradually build that up. By doing it a bit at a time, and learning to appreciate and savour the tastes you are introducing, you are better placed to stick with your new regime.

Not all fruit and vegetables are immediately palatable. Some are an acquired taste and need time to adjust to. And it is the same with your lifestyle. Choose carefully. Don't go rushing headlong to the nearest gym only to find that you can't keep going, then give up because you are embarrassed. There are plenty of exercises you can do at home that will give you a good start.

At the end of this chapter is a series of exercises that you can do in the comfort of your own home to get your exercise programme established.

Remember:

a) Eat one piece of fruit a day.

b) Eat one vegetable a day.

c) Go for a five-minute walk every day.

d) Do five minutes exercise at home every day.

Milk/water/juice

The human body can survive without food for quite a while, but it cannot survive for long without water. Water is the food of life. Just as the physical body needs water to keep it going and to avoid dehydration, so too the mental body needs its own 'water-of-life'. In fact, we need to drink the mental water of life almost as often as we need to drink water for our physical life.

To put it into perspective: the mind controls the body in everything we do. So surely we must provide it with mental nourishment. But how do we do this? Dieticians tell us to drink regularly to prevent dehydration.

And the same rule applies for your mental wellbeing. We need to regularly replenish our mental state to be able to fight off depression, anxiety and stress. And building up our mental immune system will prevent future attacks on our equilibrium.

Just as there are a whole variety of drinks on the supermarket shelf to choose from – each offering different things at different times – there are a number of ways in which we can stimulate and satisfy our mental needs.

Listed below are a variety of suggestions which you might want to consider using. As with drinks, all of them will do different things for you at different times. You will probably have to experiment to find which one, or more, suits you, but only you can decide what your mind and body needs.

Yoga	Tai Chi
Transcendental Meditation	Visualisation
Progressive Muscle Relaxation (PMR)	Reflexology
Relaxation	Massage
Indian Head Massage	Quiet time

The above list is by no means exhaustive and you are invited to try to find something that will enhance your mental wellbeing. So the next time you have a glass of water or pour yourself a soft drink, stop and think: have I taken any mental water of life today?

Bread/pasta/meat/potatoes

Most people have a main meal in the evening. Having a good meal satisfies us and makes us feel better, our energy levels are restored and we are able to start afresh.

A balanced diet can help us to offset the threat of obesity and other disorders. In the same way as a healthy meal is good for us physically, we also need a main course to help us mentally. We eat when we are physically hungry – but what do we do when we are mentally hungry?

If one of the key items is missing from any meal, it won't taste as good. And it is the same for our mental meal:

- When we're hungry we don't function as well as we should.
- When we feel hunger coming on, we can lose concentration and become a bit lethargic.
- When the brain sends a signal to remind us that we are hungry, we can't ignore it.

It is the same with our mental health. There is a constant need for mental nourishment.

If we deny our dietary needs, it affects both our physical and mental health. The groaning supermarket shelves contain a huge variety of products which we can call on when we need them. The different brands and options throughout the store allow us to dip in and out and try alternative products. And although most of us become accustomed to our favourite brands to cater for our specific tastes, we do sometimes try out the latest food promotion or recipe that is advertised on TV or in a magazine.

The many mental products available also allow us to pick and choose which one will suit our needs. We need to constantly be open to new ideas, theories, concepts and opportunities to enhance our mental health. In essence, each of us needs to become our own social scientist to become aware of what will make us happy.

Some of us make a weekly visit to the supermarket, others shop once a month. Some people stock up for days, even weeks, ahead. It should be exactly the same with our mental side. We should be planning ahead. That way we can anticipate what we might need for our mental wellbeing. We can do it with training courses, self-help groups, regular check-ups, courses and practice in mental relaxation techniques. Our aim should be to help put ourselves in a better position to deal with life's stresses and strains.

So the next time you go to the supermarket and you walk along the packed aisles, contemplating what you will buy for lunch or dinner, just take a moment to think about what 'mental' ingredients you need today. Ask yourself when and how you are going to prepare your Mental Meal.

To quote one of the country's top supermarket chains: 'Every little helps!'

Housework exercise programme

1) 20 x sit-ups

2) 20 x standing press-ups (stand, hands on wall, shoulder-width apart)

3) 20 x walk up/down stairs (if you don't have stairs, then walk around the house)

4) 20 x knee bends (hold back of chair, gently bend knees to 45 degree angle, come up slowly)

5) 20 x standing on toes (reach for top cupboard)

6) 3 x 1min walk on the spot

7) 3 x back stretching (lie on floor, stretch hands behind back as far as you can, stretch, relax, repeat)

8) 10 x r/l knee dips (stand feet slightly apart, take left leg, gently dip and lower past right knee, then repeat for right knee)

9) dishwashing blues (bend knees after washing each cup, plate, etc)

10) hoovermatic (hold on to vacuum cleaner, stand on one leg, hop as you vacuum the carpet)

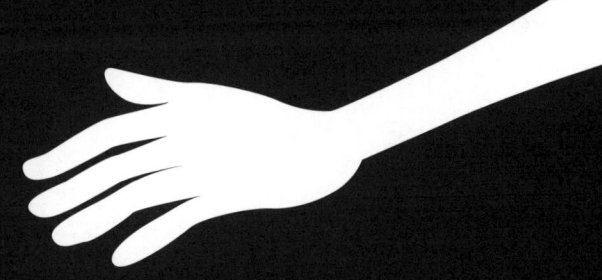

Chapter Five

Self-Esteem

Do you have a high or low opinion of yourself? Most people, when asked, would probably say that they fluctuate between high and low self-esteem. Some people believe that if you have a high opinion of yourself, you are either conceited or arrogant – or both. They rarely associate self-confidence with high self-esteem.

But having a high self-esteem and believing in yourself are vitally important. Too many of us suffer from low self-esteem, which affects our self-confidence and ability to achieve things. Your self-esteem and how you view yourself is critical to your improvement and progress as a person. After all, if you don't think you are worth very much, how do you expect others to have a high value of you?

You are a valued member of the human race, with a lot to offer. But if you continue to have a low opinion of yourself, then your true self and true potential will be lost forever.

Self-esteem is a vitally important factor in our psychological make-up. If we feel good about ourselves, we are better equipped to deal with life and life's problems, disappointments and setbacks.

Having high self-esteem does not mean that we all have to be extrovert, life-and-soul-of-the-party types. It just means that we feel good about ourselves.

Many of us frown upon those who seem to have a high opinion of themselves. We view them as arrogant and big-headed. But this stereotypical labelling is really a sad reflection on us, our cultural tradition and educational upbringing. We see these people as brash, showy and 'full of themselves' but deep down we wish we could be a bit more like them.

For example, which man would not love to carry off wearing a jacket slung casually over his shoulders like an Italian? Which female would not want to be able to wear clothes like a stylish French woman? They seem to exude so much self-esteem and self-confidence.

Unfortunately we tend to hide our self-esteem, which inhibits us and locks us into a straitjacket of dowdiness and lack of self-expression. This stifling of our self-esteem also has a detrimental effect on our mind-set.

So why do so many people have such low self-esteem? What causes it and what can be done about it?

The concept of self-esteem has considerable relevance to our everyday lives:

- It determines how we 'see' the world.
- It has an influence on our mental wellbeing.
- It is a key factor in our emotional stability and how we deal with life's demands, life satisfaction, social integration, resistance to stress and anxiety.

Being aware of yourself and having high self-esteem are important parts of your armoury, and decide who and what you are. Self-esteem is part of the continuum which is you, and is just as important as self-confidence and self-belief. It is an integral part of your being and, as such, has to be nurtured and developed.

What you feel about yourself is manifested in how you react in certain situations. High self-esteem is your passport to a better quality of life and a greater understanding of who you are.

CASE STUDY

A student came to me suffering from very low self-esteem when it came to interviews. His course work at university was fine, but when he attended job interviews he felt that he was not as good as the other candidates, particularly those from Oxbridge universities.

He believed that he was not as intelligent as them and his self-worth was at an extremely low ebb. He even attributed his own academic achievements to 'luck'!

The intervention strategy we devised was as follows:

1) Preparation:
We discussed and examined everything including his physical appearance, how to travel to interviews, what music to listen to beforehand, and we rehearsed possible questions and answers.

2) Confidence:
We discussed how to 'act' confidently. Interviews are like putting on an act for a short period of time. We prepared how he should present himself at interviews, and worked through mental rehearsals of the interview itself.

3) Dealing with nerves:
Finally we worked on how he should stay relaxed, how to control his breathing, the use of body language, and how and when to smile.

How can you improve your self-esteem? First, observe your physical appearance. As often as not, your appearance signifies so much of who you are. Far too many people don't take enough care and attention about their appearance, but it doesn't cost a lot to be smart and presentable. You don't have to spend vast amounts of money to look good.

Looking after your appearance will improve both your self-esteem and self-confidence, because we all feel psychologically better when we are well-groomed. Why don't you check out your wardrobe? There is no point in hanging on to out-of-date clothes in the hope that they will make a return and become fashionable again.

Smelling nice is also important. The scent of a nice perfume or aftershave gives you a feeling of being confident and assured. Taking time with your appearance will be re-paid many times over. To look and feel good boosts our morale and gives us confidence.

The second way to improve your self-esteem is to exercise! This is an area that frightens a lot of people. With the plethora of fitness programmes and the massive expansion in gyms and fitness clubs, it is easy to see why so many people are confused about what programme to follow and which class to join. Unfortunately many keep-fit classes put so much pressure on people that the net result is they feel uncomfortable, stop going and just return to their sedentary lifestyle.

Too many classes use training programmes which are not specific enough for the individual. The classes are 'one-fit' for everybody, which means the ones who can't keep up feel they've failed and just give up.

It is not easy for everyone to go and join a gym – some people are too self-conscious about their weight, shape or general lack of fitness. A much simpler approach is to try a programme of walking and gentle exercises, which can easily be done within the confines of your own home. This will allow you to make steady progress, which will build up your fitness levels and enhance your self-esteem. (Try the simple exercise programme at the end of the previous chapter.)

Feeling healthy makes you more mentally alert, improves your outlook on life and helps you cope much better with the ups and downs of daily living. Embarking on a personalised fitness programme is important for your life, irrespective of what age you are.

CASE STUDY

A top amateur golfer had such low self-esteem that he maintained all his good results were the product of external factors, like poor opposition and being lucky. Even when he achieved a round of 65, he would maintain that he had played badly. He always felt intimidated among other top golfers, especially professionals, because he did not believe that his success was down to his ability.

Our intervention strategy:

1) Performance Focus:
The player was taught how to focus on his performance and not on 'external' factors.

2) Imagery:
He was taught the mental skills of using imagery to project himself – to himself and others – in a better light.

3) Self-Talk:
The player was introduced to the skill of using 'Positive Self-Talk' to remind himself of his value as a human being and as a golfer.

Some form of physical exercise is good for everyone, and although many people have been living a sedentary life for far too long, it is never too late to start. However, before you begin any fitness programme, you should always have a medical check-up with your GP or health professional. Once you have been given the all-clear to start exercising, it is imperative that you start slowly and carefully. Those who start with great gusto and enthusiasm soon find that they have overdone it and end up either injured or giving up altogether.

And there are so many benefits:

- Feeling physically good about yourself makes you feel mentally good about yourself.
- It improves your self-esteem and makes you feel more comfortable with who you are.
- Your clothes seem to fit better.
- You will smile a lot more.
- You become more tolerant and patient.
- You can concentrate better and for longer.
- You become less aggressive, because being physically active allows you to get rid of pent-up anger and emotions in a safe and controlled manner.

Life seems much better when we are physically in good shape. Our appetite improves and many people report that they sleep better. So, to improve our self-esteem we need some form of physical activity on a daily basis. We don't need to run ourselves into the ground, but we do need to be committed to exercising daily. The length of time we exercise is entirely up to each individual. For some people who have not done any exercise for many years, a simple five-minute walk is a good place to start, or a five-minute swim is just as beneficial. There is no point in pushing yourself too hard too soon.

The key to successful exercising is consistency. It is easier to start with a five-minute programme than a 30–45 minute programme. There is nothing more soul-destroying than having to give up because the programme was too hard early on. So think seriously before you start. It's not too much to take just five minutes out of your day, but it might be too much to take 30–45 minutes. Once a year everyone should have a physical MOT and take the expert medical advice regarding our physical wellbeing. But that five minutes out of your day, every day, will begin to keep the engine of your life ticking over.

CASE STUDY

A professional footballer came to me with extremely low self-esteem. He had been released by a premier league club and, with no club to go to, was desperate for my help.

Our intervention strategy:

1) Goal-setting. We sat down and made plans for the next one, three and five years.

2) The player signed up with a football agent.

3) He obtained a contract.

4) We introduced Mental Skills Training, including visualisation skills, confidence building, anger management, how to deal with setbacks and disappointments and building self-belief.

5) He became the captain of his new club.

6) He went on to win 40 international caps for his country.

The third – and final – piece of the self-esteem jigsaw is what we eat. Begin today and start to modify what you eat and the amount that you consume. If you're not sure, there are plenty of dietary articles, books and DVDs available, or you could consult your GP or a medical professional. Remember the old saying we mentioned earlier:

'Inch by inch
It's a cinch.
Yard by yard
It's too hard.'

You have the power within you to change – so DO IT!

What and how much you eat have a direct bearing on your self-esteem. If you do not eat the right things, it will have a detrimental effect on your lifestyle. Every day we are bombarded with information regarding our diet and what we should and shouldn't eat. However, the maxim 'garbage in, garbage out' perfectly applies to our eating habits.

We all know that we should eat the right types of food, but not all of us can afford to. Advertisements bombard us with 'expert' advice and opinions, from eating five pieces of fruit a day to reducing our calorific intake. Sometimes it is difficult to know what to do and what to choose, or who to listen to.

But there are certain undisputable facts which are not challenged. Generally speaking:

- We do not eat enough fruit/veg.
- We eat far too many frozen/convenience meals.
- We buy too many takeaways.

The subsequent rise in obesity is alarming. What we eat and how much we eat directly affects our moods, emotions, personality and self-esteem.

Diets low in fats, saturated fats, salt and cholesterol can reduce the risk of cancer, heart disease and obesity.

Diets low in sodium can reduce high blood pressure and strokes, while diets high in fruit, vegetables and whole grains can reduce the risk of cancer.

For general eating guidelines, the following may be of assistance:

1) Set up a time schedule for meals. Sit down to eat in a quiet, enjoyable atmosphere.

2) Always eat a healthy breakfast.

3) Be aware of what you are eating. Check portion sizes – read the labels.

4) Instead of eating when you are bored or stressed, do some exercises.

5) Reward yourself with a sauna, massage, etc, if you lose weight.

6) For long-term weight control, exercise and healthy eating are the only solutions.

7) Eat slowly, enjoy your meal and, if possible, the company.

8) Drink a glass of water with your meal.

9) Take fruit as a snack.

10) Eat at least one portion of fruit a day (it's a start!).

11) Eat to enjoy.

Your self-esteem is a product of all three aspects outlined in this chapter:

- You are what you eat!
- You look how you dress!
- You think how you feel!

All three are interconnected and if one is out of kilter, the effect will be felt on your self-esteem. How do you feel about yourself right now? Are you happy with what you see when you look in the mirror? Does your reflection inspire or disgust you? Do you want to change your appearance? Your weight? Your physical shape? Does the way you feel about yourself hold you back from being who you want to be?

There is no better time to:

- have a better opinion about yourself
- build your self-esteem
- stop wallowing in the sea of self-pity and negative thinking
- start believing in yourself a bit more

Yes, the forces of negativity and doubt are hard forces to overcome – but it can be done! The next time you look in the mirror, just remember that the biggest obstacle to improving your self-esteem is staring right back at you!

CASE STUDY

An international netball player was so low in self-esteem that she believed everything she did was wrong.

She was convinced she was not tall enough, slim enough, athletic enough or even as pretty as other members of the team. And being substituted only exacerbated the situation and lowered her value of herself.

Our intervention:

1) The player was taught how to analyse her performance with the skill of Detailed Reflection and to highlight which were the good parts of her game and which parts needed refining.

2) Confidence Counselling Sessions.

3) Mental Skills Training.

4) Self-worth.

5) Positive Self-talk/Positive Performance focus.

6) The eradication of negative thoughts and anxiety.

If you can overcome YOU and your negative thoughts on a daily basis, then you have a chance of winning the battle of low self-esteem. If you don't have a high opinion of yourself, how do you expect others to have one of you?

You are a unique person. There is nobody quite like you in the world. Nobody laughs like you, talks like you, walks like you, thinks like you, acts like you. The only time that is relevant is now! By unlocking the chains that hold you back, you can come to terms with the present and face the future with greater hope and determination.

How you feel about yourself will determine your present and future actions, hopes and aspirations. Be confident in who you are and disregard any negative comments that other people make about you. All of us at one time or another have had our self-esteem challenged, abused, derided, criticised or mocked. These can be very hurtful experiences and can take a long time to recover from – but it can be done. Far too often we allow ourselves to be put off, to underachieve because of a put-down or a derogatory remark. But we must learn to rise above these comments.

In the final analysis, it's what you think about yourself that really matters. If you work hard at changing your self-esteem, you will succeed.

- Work at it on a daily basis.
- Don't give in, don't give up.
- You will come through a better, stronger person.
- You owe it to yourself – nobody else – to be the person you have always wanted to be.
- Don't let anyone steal your dreams.
- Don't let anyone tell you that you do not have the ability to achieve this or that.
- You have a right to dream.
- You have a right to turn those dreams into reality.

The only question you have to ask yourself is: what is stopping you? Be proud of yourself!

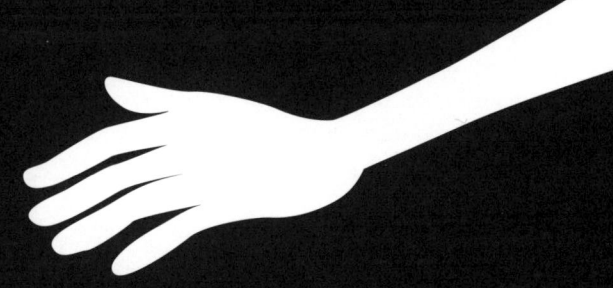

Chapter Six

Are You Self-Confident?

Do you believe you have abilities and qualities that other people don't have? Do you really believe that you have the confidence to succeed? Having belief in yourself and being self-confident are necessary ingredients for your success. Without self-confidence you won't progress. Developing a strong sense of confidence will allow you to achieve your goals, recover from setbacks and disappointments, and make you more determined. If you have limited self-confidence, you will have limited success. If, on the other hand, you have a strong sense of confidence allied with determination, then you will succeed.

Unfortunately no-one can give you self-confidence – but they can help. Self-confidence is 'internal', a feeling. But we can take inspiration and advice from others. We can use the concept of 'role models' and apply that to making us believe in ourselves a bit more and follow the examples of other successful people.

How often have you heard it said that somebody lacked self-confidence? Sports commentators and team managers are always using this type of language. The question is – how do they know? What are the signs? How is a lack of self-confidence displayed?

Let's start at the beginning. You know you had a certain amount of self-confidence when you were younger – otherwise you would not have achieved as much as you have already. The facts speak for themselves. You can ride a bike, swim, drive a car, etc. To achieve any one of those skills requires a level of self-confidence. And these skills can be added to.

Just take a moment to write down all that you have achieved so far. Now that you have done that, ask yourself why and how you achieved them. The next question to ask is – why can't I add more skills? What's stopping me? Where has my self-confidence gone? It may be that an external event has prevented you from developing your self-confidence. But whatever the blockages are, they are not insurmountable.

Self-confidence cannot be bought in a store! It is something you have to work at internally. It is true that some people always appear more self-confident than others. But too many people are discouraged from truly believing in themselves and as a result do not fulfil their true potential. If we are put down and subjected to negative comments, we do not develop sufficient self-confidence in ourselves and settle for mediocrity instead. It's time to start to be self-confident and dismiss your doubters. Take great pleasure in doing the things other people say you can't do. That alone will kick-start your sense of self-confidence.

How often have you watched someone perform at the top of their sport, business or profession and marvelled at how easy they make it look and how confident they look? The question is – were they always like that or did they acquire self-confidence? It might surprise you to know that a lot of famous people were not that self-confident at first. Indeed many of them 'acted' confidently until they 'became' confident.

So just what is self-confidence? And how will you recognise that you have it? Basically it is a belief and trust in your own abilities/skills/talents and being sure of oneself. Self-confidence is having complete trust in you. As we are all products of our own environments and experiences, it is these that shape how we view the world and how we interact with it.

We are conditioned and influenced by early life experiences that shape our behaviour and our personality. If our parents were lacking in self-confidence, the chances are we will be as well. If you are constantly given negative comments and feedback in school, you will come to accept those negative comments and become less self-confident. And once the forces of negativity have taken hold, it is extremely difficult to break out of them. But it's not impossible!

With self-confidence:

- We are able to face the disappointments and setbacks life throws at us.
- We experience a sense of being self-assured, and our level of performance increases.
- We feel better about ourselves and believe we can make a contribution.
- We go into situations with a better level of expectation and outcome.
- We interact better and the quality of our life improves.

If the opposite is true, we become more pessimistic and our expectations are low. When we don't handle disappointments or rejection properly, we become withdrawn and shy away from interaction with other people.

At various times in our lives, we will undoubtedly experience rejection. This may take the form of emotional rejection, family rejection, employment rejection, friendship rejection, team rejection and so on. How we deal with that and come to terms with it mentally, will determine what kind of self-confidence we have. Nobody likes rejection of any kind, but it is something that we may have to face up to. Sometimes it can make us more determined, so the rejection is used as a catalyst for further action. For others the pain is too great and there is a tendency to retreat, to withdraw and to give up. In simple terms it is 'Flight or Fight' – the choice is yours.

Opening a letter that says you have not been successful in a job application can have a devastating effect on your self-confidence – especially if it is one of many. Being told that you have not passed your exams, driving test, or whatever, can have a demoralising impact on your self-confidence and push it to the point of despair.

Emotional rejection is also painful to deal with. By its very nature it is a very 'personal' experience, which only the individual can have. We all deal with these issues in our own way. Some people deal with them by themselves and call on their inner-strength, some enlist the aid of family and friends, and others may use the professional psychological services. But dealing with the situation will have an impact on our self-confidence.

We marvel at the way some people appear able to bounce back effortlessly from any kind of rejection. But you should remember some of us are better than others at disguising our pain. Don't be fooled by their act or masquerade – they will be hurting, but their self-confidence and inner-strength will see them through.

The issue for you is how you handle these situations. How are you going to deal with situations that directly challenge your self-confidence? These may be work-related, emotionally or family-related. Dealing with them will determine your future level of self-confidence and progress as an individual.

Having complete trust in your abilities/skills/talents and mental toughness is central to your self-confidence. When your confidence is threatened or questioned, it is easy to become anxious, stressed and doubtful about your ability to cope. This can ultimately lead to a serious situation where you allow the feelings of rejection, disappointment and doubt to overwhelm you.

There are simple things we can do to put things into perspective and maintain our self-confidence. If we rationalise what has happened, we are in a better position to deal with adverse situations when they arise. Developing a mental strength will enable you to overcome those disappointments. The following list includes some ideas/suggestions you might want to consider and act on to make you more mentally strong:

- One of the ways to consider responding is to 'act' confidently, even though you may not feel it. Take going for an interview for a job, for instance. Most people feel a little anxious and nervous prior to the actual interview, which is perfectly normal and healthy. Having a few nerves is not a bad thing. The problem arises when the anxiety/nerves become too great and threaten to affect our performance.

- Going for an interview is like an actor going on stage. Before an actor steps on stage, he/she has to learn the lines and rehearse the part they are going to be playing. And so can you! You can rehearse your answers prior to the interview. You can imagine, visualise and rehearse the type of questions that you are likely to be asked.

- By mentally rehearsing the interview, and visualising as much detail as possible – where the interview is to be held, the surroundings, how you will get there, the time you arrive, etc – you will be thoroughly prepared. By the time you actually get there, you will already have gone through the interview and will feel a lot more confident in the process. Going for an interview is like being in the final of a major race. There can only be one winner – make sure it's YOU!

CASE STUDY

Sally Gunnell, the 1992 Olympic Champion in the 400m hurdles, still uses visualisation even though her athletic career is over. Now a motivational speaker, she is quoted in Jeff Grout and Sarah Perrin's book *Mind Games* as saying, 'I use it when I am giving a talk before 5000 people. This scared the life out of me, but I visualised myself standing on the stage, delivering the perfect speech and people enjoying what I was saying. It really helped and allowed me to control my nerves. I visualise myself beforehand, talking and feeling confident.'

There are plenty of books written about how to conduct yourself at interviews and the psychology of interviewing. But too many people fail at interviews, not because of lack of ability or not having enough qualifications, but because they did not prepare properly. They lose out because they appear to lack self-confidence. The signals that you send through your body language have a bearing on the interview, so rehearsing body language should be considered. Take into account that the people who are interviewing you may also be a bit anxious and nervous. By rehearsing your body language, your responses, the level/pitch of your voice, you stand a better chance of being successful.

- Rehearse your responses in front of a mirror.
- Time your answers.
- Practise your body language.

Don't be one of those interviewees who answer a question at an interview quicker than Usain Bolt ran the 100 metres final in Beijing, ie 9.65 seconds!

There are things you cannot control, such as the weather or the interviewing panel, but you can control your attitude, your determination, your desire and your approach. Try to remember how confident you felt in the past when you achieved something. Is there any reason why you can't get that feeling back again? The short answer is NO! By constantly reminding yourself of successful things you have achieved in the past and dismissing all negative thinking, you can regain a positive outlook and be self-confident.

As with so many things in life, self-confidence is a state of mind which begins and ends there. The trick is to conquer and control the mind, and the way we 'talk' to ourselves is the key.

- Do you really believe in yourself?
- Do you tell yourself inwardly that you can make a contribution, that you can be successful?
- Do you remind yourself constantly that you are a worthy person, a valued human being and a confident person?

Nothing comes easy but if you work hard enough at it, your self-confidence can improve. There will be occasions when it will desert you, but you must believe that you can get it back. Temporary blips are quite common and no cause to panic. Very few people are self-confident all the time. Sometimes we feel a little bit apprehensive, a little bit insecure, a little less sure about ourselves. If you feel like that, relax – you are in good company! The real problem arises when we allow our emotions and feelings of uncertainty to overwhelm us and prevent us from functioning at our best.

Try smiling as a way of showing you're self-confident. If we smile a lot, people associate that as being confident and gravitate towards us. If, on the other hand, we are frowning and look miserable, then we are likely to be on our own. 'Smiling adds to your face value!' Even a nervous smile is better than no smile at all.

In essence, there are ten aspects to your self-confidence. By following and adopting some, if not all, of the suggestions, you are well on your way to conquering your lack of confidence:

1) ACT Self-Confidence:

This has been mentioned before but it is worth repeating. Acting self-confidence will ultimately make you feel self-confident. By acting, you are rehearsing that part. We are all actors at different times and on different occasions. By acting self-confident, you will become self-confident – then you won't need to act!

2) SMILE Self-Confidence:

We give an air of self-confidence when we smile. It makes other people happy and they will smile back at us. Smiling puts people at ease and allows you the opportunity to interact better with other people. It gives them a feeling of warmth, security and a feeling that you are interested in them. Having the confidence to smile is the key to opening many doors.

3) REHEARSE/PRACTISE Self-Confidence:

When we rehearse something we become better at it. Remember the saying 'Practice makes perfect'? Well, it should be 'Practice makes *permanent*'. Whatever challenge you face, if you rehearse and practise, you will be in better shape to deal with your lack of self-confidence.

4) VISUALISE/IMAGINE Self-Confidence:

All of us have dreamt at one time or another about being a famous film-star, musician, footballer, singer or artist. Dreams are important to us, yet few of us turn our dreams into reality. We don't use our imagination or visualisation skills to the full. Many top class athletes and business people use imagery/visualisation skills to go over their performance and help them prepare for competition. It helps them with their confidence and is a skill that you can acquire with practice. Most Olympic and world class athletes will spend at least 15–20 minutes a day visualising their performance and preparing for competition. If you want to improve your level of self-confidence, you should start to visualise yourself in different settings. It's like watching yourself on a TV screen, except you can decide which channel you want to watch. Once you have developed your imagery/visualisation skills, you will realise that they can be replayed in real-life situations. It's as if you have already been there and gradually your self-confidence will emerge stronger than before. Using your mental skills in this way is a positive way to overcome your lack of confidence.

CASE STUDY

Louis Ferrigno, the actor best known for his role as the Incredible Hulk, had a rough start in life. He explains: 'When I was three years old, I had a bad ear infection that caused me to lose 75% of my hearing. The other kids called me "Deaf Louie" or "the Mute". I escaped with comic books. Those were my happy times, reading about Superman and the Incredible Hulk. I'd read and read and memorise the words and actions of characters like the Incredible Hulk, then I'd imagine myself big and strong and heroic. I was about 12 when I was using my father's weights.

'When I wasn't reading about my heroes, I was working out to become like my heroes. I won the Mr. Universe competition when I was 21. I was asked to audition for the role of the Incredible Hulk (TV series) and I went down for the screen test. They liked the way that I showed my emotions without speaking. My hearing loss made me unique in that way, in that character role. I knew the Hulk very well since my childhood of reading comic books. In a way I had been preparing for this role for many years. That changed my whole life. It was like a dream come true.' (E. Suss, *When Hearing Gets Hard*, Bantam Books, 1993)

5) THINK Self-Confidence:

People often talk about something being a 'self-fulfilling prophecy'. What they mean by this is that if you constantly 'think' you have low self-confidence then that is exactly what you will have! How often have you heard that somebody had a 'feeling' they were going to under-perform, lose a match, fail an exam, etc? If you keep thinking in negative terms, the chances are you will be a negative person – your glass will always look half-empty instead of half-full. Thinking positively is infinitely better than having negative thoughts. The second a negative thought comes into your head, you should immediately switch your thoughts to something positive, like using your remote to change the channel on your TV. Thoughts control the mind, how we are going to behave, what our actions are going to be, or how we are going to respond to certain situations. But if we can control our thinking, we have a chance of improving our self-confidence. It is an internal issue. Environmental factors can influence our self-confidence, but they do not have to control it. We don't have to let them dominate or master our response. Change your 'I can't' to 'I WILL!'

Stop thinking about what you don't want and start thinking what you do want. Lack of self-confidence is usually the product of some negative experience that has lodged itself in your subconscious mind and stayed there. All your thought processes regarding confidence are then negative and you convince yourself that you can't do anything about it. Such negative thinking is harmful to your development as a person, so it is important that you make a start in the way that you think about yourself.

Take control of your thought processes and don't allow the dark forces of negative thoughts to take hold and prevent you from moving forward. Start thinking you are confident and you'll soon begin to believe you are. Break down the word CONFIDENCE to CON-fidence: that three-letter word CON means a 'trick'. And that's exactly what you have to do to your thought process – you have to CON (or trick) it into thinking that you're confident! It won't happen overnight. The change you are looking for is a gradual process.

6) TALK Self-Confidence:

Everybody talks to themselves. When we are thinking about something, we're actually talking to ourselves. Don't worry, the men in white coats won't be coming to take you away. It is a perfectly natural thing to do. The only problem is that many of us talk to ourselves in a negative way. To start turning things around, we need to begin talking positively to ourselves.

Instead of hearing your inner-voice saying, 'I can't do that – I'm not capable' you have to change it to say: 'I can do that – I'm capable of doing it. I will do that!' Say it often enough and your self-confidence will grow. It may take some time but if you persevere with changing your inner-voice, it will eventually say more positive things to you than negative. All of us at one time or another will use a phrase like 'Give yourself a shake!' to encourage ourselves to perform better at a particular situation, skill or task. This same principle can be applied to creating a form of words that will help us to be more self-confident. We can overcome a whole variety of issues by talking to ourselves in a positive manner. Start to talk yourself 'up' – self-defeating talk only brings you down.

7) MODEL Self-Confidence:

Who are your heroes and why? Who inspires you? When we were young many of us would model ourselves on a famous film/TV star, footballer or pop singer. Having heroes or models we can look up to can inspire us and help us with our self-confidence. They don't even have to be famous. By modelling yourself on someone you admire, you can imagine how they would handle the situation you are in. Some people have used comedians as a vehicle for overcoming a particular phobia like flying. This may work for some people, but in more severe cases professional help is required.

Even famous people have a similar approach, by modelling themselves on their heroes. Think about the people who inspire you: what is it they do that you admire? Are there any particular qualities, skills or talents they have which you like? Do they have a certain way of walking or talking? Do they carry themselves well and exude an air of confidence? Are they able to hide their nervousness better than you? Do you wish you could be like them? If the answer is yes – try to copy some of their attributes into your own behaviour. If life is an act, why don't you act self-confidently? Just as you can learn new skills, so you have to work at modelling your self-confidence. Take a stroll down the catwalk of self-confidence.

8) KEEP PRACTISING Self-Confidence:

There is no such thing as perfection. Perfection is something that we all aspire to but never reach. But if we practise something long enough, we can make that skill or technique permanent. When we were young and started to learn how to ride a bike, to swim or to drive a car, we made a lot of mistakes. Yet through perseverance, determination and practice, we gradually reduced those errors and mastered that particular skill. And the mastery of the skill became permanent. Once we learnt it, we could not unlearn it.

This same principle can be applied to being more self-confident. If we practise enough at being self-confident, eventually we will become more self-confident. Start by:

- making a list of those areas/situations where you feel less self-confident
- choosing one item from that list
- identifying areas that you could improve on
- practising those areas of improvement
- trying out this new approach in real-life situations
- keep practising until you've mastered it, then move onto the next one on your list

There are so many skills which we now take for granted, yet they all had to be learned and practised. Achieving self-confidence is no different.

9) BELIEVE in your Self-Confidence:

Do you truly believe in yourself? Do you feel that you have abilities, skills and talents that other people don't have? Do you really believe you have the confidence to succeed? Having belief in yourself is a necessary ingredient for your success and personal development. Without self-belief, you will not make the progress you are capable of. If, on the other hand, you have limited self-belief you will have limited achievement. How often have you heard it said that someone lacked 'self-belief'? Commentators at sporting events forever make this claim.

Believe it or not, you had a great amount of self-belief and self-confidence when you were younger. Write down all that you have achieved so far. Then ask yourself why you can't go on to believe in yourself to achieve much more. It could be that some external circumstances are holding you back or blocking your path. Whatever the blockages, they are not insurmountable. Belief in yourself cannot be bought in a shop! You have to work at it inside your head. It is a constant daily battle that you have to win.

Why do you think Barack Obama is now the 44th President of the USA? He believed in himself and had supreme self-confidence in his abilities. If you do not start to truly believe in yourself, you will not realise your full potential. You have to rise above those put-downs and voices of negativity. If you don't, you subject yourself to a life of mediocrity.

- Start to believe in yourself and dismiss all the doubters.
- Take great pleasure in doing the things that other people said you couldn't do!
- Begin to truly believe in yourself and watch yourself develop and grow.
- Watch how your horizons will stretch out before you and new ones will come into view.
- Help yourself to some of that self-belief and self-confidence.
- Stop wallowing in the sea of self-pity.
- Prove to yourself – no-one else – that you are capable of achieving many things in your life.

It won't be easy and sometimes the going will get tough, but think of the fun and enjoyment you'll have on the journey of self-development. Don't be one of those who give up too early because the going gets tough. Stay with your dreams, ideals and goals. Work at them; don't let them wither on the vine. You have it in you to change.

10) BE Self-Confident:

It is easier said than done to 'be' self-confident. This chapter has highlighted some of the ways that you may want to consider improving your self-confidence. Nobody likes to be in a situation where they feel nervous. We feel better when we are confident. We feel able to do things and are more comfortable within ourselves. Being self-confident adds to our feeling of self-esteem. We feel mentally in control, safe and confident within ourselves. Being confident means we are more able to deal with life's disappointments, setbacks and challenges, and can bounce back.

Being self-confident is a state of mind. You can decide to be either confident or not confident. You can decide that you will or you won't do something. You can either rise to the challenge of life, or decide not to bother. Follow the examples of those people whom you admire or who inspire you. Take a leaf out of their book. Look at their life stories, how they have developed as a person and how self-confident they are. If they can do it, why can't you?

Be the person you have always wanted to be. Make a start today.

- Remind yourself to be confident.
- Write down daily 'I Am Confident!'
- Keep writing this every day until you finally believe it.
- Keep working on that unquenchable desire to be confident.
- Be mentally strong and learn how to use disappointments and setbacks as learning episodes to make you stronger.
- Walk tall. If you are 5ft 6ins, then walk 5ft 8ins!
- Hold your head high.
- Add some bright colours to your wardrobe.
- Practise giving a warm, firm handshake.
- Start to smile a little more every day. Smiling makes you look confident.

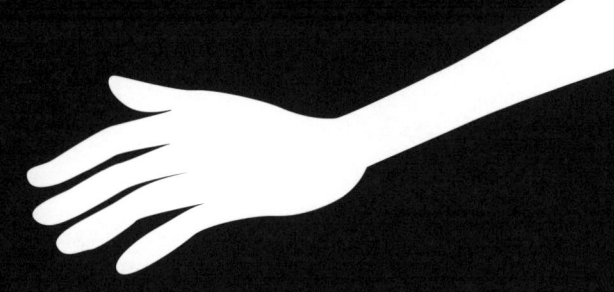

Chapter Seven

The Open Self

They say that life imitates sport and sport imitates life. Take the analogy between golf and life, for instance, and imagine that life is like a set of golf clubs. When a golfer opens up his (or her) bag, there are some 14 clubs to choose from. Some will be used more than others, but each one is important and will be called upon at certain times. However, without detailed knowledge of each club and its purpose, a golfer will not be able to navigate his way successfully around the course. The Open Self mirrors golf and life. The clubs are:

1) The Driver:
Used at the beginning of every game, by and large the driver is used for nearly every hole. So the execution of a good drive is vitally important to get off to a good start. Likewise in life, it is important that we work on our Self-Driver. It is the one that will open the fairway ahead. You can stand on the first tee and see the target far away in the distance. You know that you can't reach it in one shot, but you also know that if you hit it straight down the middle you will be in a good position to reach the pinhole. You may have some idea of where you want to go or be, and you can see it in your mind's eye. But unless you drive yourself at it, the chances are you might end up in the rough. By using your own 'self-drive' to accurately hit the road ahead, you will be able to navigate yourself around the course of life.

2) The Putter:
Next to the driver, the putter is perhaps the most used and most important club in a golfer's bag. The putter is designed for accuracy and delicate touch. The use of the putter also demands full concentration and composure in order to put the ball into the hole. Sometimes the distance can be very short – like six inches – and sometimes it can be very long, perhaps 25–30 metres. When we start out on our journey through the Open of Life, we need to be like the putter. We need to concentrate fully on what we are doing and what we want to achieve. Your commitment to your goal in life will depend on how well you can putt the ball, so you need to be composed and concentrate fully on what you are doing. To make a successful putt takes time; it is a slow, methodical process. Golfers only putt when they are ready and have examined the shot from all angles. It is important that you do the same when making decisions that will affect your life. Then, when you are ready, execute the process. When a golfer holes a putt there is no greater feeling. When you reach one of your goals, you will feel the same.

3) The Sand Wedge:
A round of golf does not always run smoothly. Sometimes the ball does not go where you want it to go. Every now and then you will hit a stray shot and it will end up in the bunker. Life is also like that. Sometimes the road we are on suddenly changes and we find ourselves lost. The golfer,

although angry with himself, will have practised for such an event. He will have rehearsed for such an occasion, both technically and mentally, and will know how to get out of a bunker. Using the sand wedge, he will have practised this situation many times. Many golfers use the 'what if' approach to difficult shots. They look at every possible scenario before making a decision about which type of shot they will make. The 'what if' approach is useful in life, as it will enable you to look at difficult situations and find a way through them. The sand wedge is specifically designed to help a golfer out of a difficult situation. Like a golfer, you need a mental strategy to get you out of a difficult situation. By using your 'Open Self' you make yourself available for help. Far too many of us bottle up our anxieties and worries. By being 'open' the chances are that somebody or something will be there to help and assist us. Don't be afraid to be more 'open' with yourself and confide in those people who have your best interests at heart. Use your mental sand wedge to prise open your need to share your worries, anxieties and fears with someone close to you. Like a golfer, you can find yourself going astray and perhaps ending up in the bunker of life. To get out, you need a plan of action:

- assess the problem
- look for options
- choose a course of action
- carry out your decision
- review the decision

4) The Fairway Woods:

The 3 and 5 fairway woods are usually used by golfers for long shots. They require both power and accuracy. This is also true of your 'Open Self'. You require power to stay the course and accuracy in assessing your decisions. You also need power to overcome those negative things that get in the way. We are all asked for and demand accuracy in so many aspects of our lives. We require accuracy in our bills, in our dealings with shops and businesses, and we have to be accurate with information regarding our personal life. So you need to be absolutely clear about what you want in life. Start by working on those simple aspects of your daily life that are a distraction and be more accurate in dealing with them. By doing so, you will be able to take more control over your own life.

5) The Long Irons:

The 2, 3, and 4 irons are classed by golfers as 'long' irons and are used in the same way as the fairway woods, ie with power and accuracy. In golf, different clubs are used for different purposes. In life, different solutions and remedies are needed to tackle the many and varied daily scenarios that you find yourself in. No two shots are the same in golf, just as there are no two problems which have the same solution. In real life we use a variety of methods and decisions, depending on the circumstances that we find ourselves in. Like in golf, we should see every potential problem as a 'challenge' to our ability to find a solution. The challenge to every golfer is to beat the course. The challenge for you is to open yourself up to the many opportunities that life will present to you. Golfers don't give up just because they hit a bad shot, have a poor round, or don't make the cut. They re-group, re-focus, refresh themselves and go again. This is what you have to do when things are not going well. Don't give up!

6) The Mid Irons:

The 5, 6, and 7 irons are classed as mid irons in golf. They require a more delicate touch, allied with some power. This tussle between power and accuracy/delicacy is reminiscent of what happens in real-life situations. The decision a golfer has to make is based on certain information at his disposal, taking into account the distance for the shot, the environment, the difficulty of the shot, the percentage of success/failure, the weather. All of these factors are considered and assessed before a club is selected. Likewise, your Open Self needs to be aware of all the information necessary for you to make decisions regarding your own life. It is up to you to make those decisions – and you alone. You can listen to informed opinion and assess all the information that you can get, but ultimately it is down to you which decisions you make. When you open yourself up to the possibilities that lie before you, a fundamental change will take place. Your conscious decision to make a change in your life will require you to embrace that change, and that change will be endemic in your life. All of us get older and less mobile, but what so many of us fail to grasp is that we also mentally change. Life is a daily mental battle to be won. As we get older and – like the golfer – further round the course, we require more mental and physical staying power. Adapting to life's changes can be a hard thing to do, but we can prepare for it and embrace it better than we currently do. Changing anything is not easy. It is hard for someone who has been a smoker for a number of years to suddenly stop. Despite all the health warnings on the packet and the associated risks, many people find it difficult to have the staying power to give up. Yet there is one simple solution to this problem. Don't buy cigarettes! At first glance, that may seem too simplistic and unrealistic. On closer examination the vital question is: how serious are people when they say they want to give up smoking? If the answer is very – then stop actually buying them. It's a case of mind over habit! To kick the habit, smokers first have to have the willpower to want to give up, then find the route to giving up. And it's the same with any change in your life.

7) The Short Irons:

The 8 and 9 irons are generally called the short irons in golf, and are usually used for accuracy and controlled distance. Golfers, therefore, have to be in control – physically, mentally and technically. If any one of the three components is out of sync, the shot may be affected. Golfers rely very much on being in control of their game. But they can't control everything. They can't control the weather, the shape of the course, their opponents or the crowd. What they can control is their attitude, their commitment and their determination. This also applies to your life. You have to take control of your Open Self and whatever it is you want to achieve. Whatever it is you are doing, you must do it to the best of your ability. Take control of the things you can control and don't worry about the things that you can't. Like the golfer, focus only on what you can control.

Look at the choices you have to make, look at the physical changes you want to make, and look at the outcome you want. Too many golfers worry about their game, particularly if they make a mess of a shot. But worry doesn't solve anything, and the more we worry about things the less we act on them. Like the golfer, you may end up not only in the rough but taking too many shots, or even out of bounds. The trick is to stop digging a bigger hole for yourself, get out of the rough and back onto the fairway. Golf's step-by-step approach will stand you in good stead in life. No problem will seem insurmountable, no disappointment too great to recover from, no setback too severe to overcome. Look at life's trials like a game of golf, and get out there and enjoy the fresh air! Enjoy what life has to offer you. As you stand on the first tee and look out onto the fairway of your life, pause for a moment and remind yourself how wonderful life is.

CASE STUDY

A young professional golfer came to see me regarding his mental approach to his game. He felt that he was 'lost' out on the course and could not see a way out of the slump he was currently experiencing. His poor performances were having an adverse effect on other parts of his life.

He practised hard every day and his training regime included a lot of gym work. On average he would hit over 3000 balls per week. But his short game was poor and his confidence low, especially in tournaments. He admitted he could not deal with hitting a 'bad' stroke and was always looking for the 'perfect' shot. It was clear that he was placing a terrible burden on himself, to such an extent that he was no longer enjoying his golf. The slightest distraction or negative thought made him play badly. He could even predict how well/badly he was going to play after only his first tee shot!

Our programme involved spending a lot of time discussing his training regime, his approach to competition and how he lived his life. He accepted that his 'chaotic' lifestyle was holding him back and not allowing him to perform at his best consistently.

The first thing that we changed was his training regime. A carefully planned and organised weekly regime was introduced, with the help of his golf coach, and his training became more specific and detailed. A Mental Skills training programme was introduced to include such topics as:

a) distraction control

b) concentration

c) relaxation control

d) preparation for competition

e) recovery procedures during competition

f) planning/preparing to perform

g) pre/post shot routines

We agreed that other topics would be added later. After a period of several months, he is now a more assured, confident and smiling professional golfer.

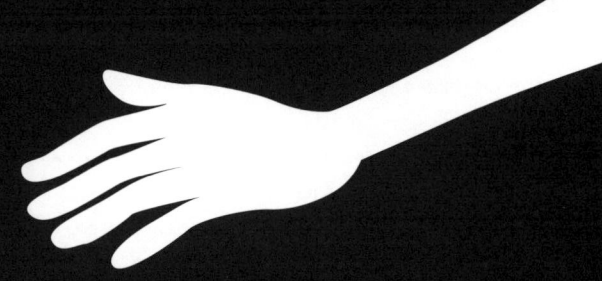

Chapter Eight

Shout For Your Self

Have you ever heard yourself shout? There are times when we have to shout to be heard, especially in a crowded room, a noisy pub or at a concert. Sometimes it feels that the only way to get noticed is by shouting.

Nobody likes to be ignored, but far too often we find ourselves locked into a silent, deprecating world. We seem almost invisible and allow things and people to walk all over us. Our resistance is low, our self-esteem has gone into hiding and we would rather retreat and slip away into the background than face up to life's injustices. We don't complain when we are served a poor meal, receive poor service or are totally ignored. We don't seem to be able to stand up for ourselves.

If all of this applies to you, there is a simple solution – SHOUT for your Self internally! It is not a vocal response that you need. You need to shout inside that you are refusing to accept things as they are. Think of yourself as a volcano just before it erupts, and start to put those vital changes into effect. Otherwise, like the volcano, you will eventually blow your top and scatter your efforts all over the place. Ideally you want to deal with any situation or conflict before it gets too critical, so 'shouting' for yourself is really you standing up for your Self.

- Don't wait until things get on top of you.
- Don't wait until you get yourself into a situation where you feel you can't react, are not in control or feel helpless.
- Storing things up only breeds negative feelings and doubts.
- Be more pro-active and begin to redress the balance.

Start by rehearsing out loud how you are going to act in a certain situation. For example, take that awkward telephone call that you have been putting off. Why not write down what you want to say/ask? Rehearse those questions out loud. You are now more likely to have the confidence to ask/say those things than if you go on the phone cold and unprepared.

Hearing the sound of your own voice and making it strong will allow you to 'shout' even louder for yourself. It is a sign of inner-strength and confidence. Not all of us have the confidence and skills to deal with awkward or tricky situations. But by preparing and rehearsing to 'shout' for ourselves, we are in a much better position to be in control. How often have you come off the phone or left a meeting and wished you had had the confidence to ask certain questions or put points across? How often have you been in a situation where you have been fobbed off and treated in a shabby fashion, yet lacked the voice to respond in a strong and positive manner?

All too often we put up with poor service owing to a lack of self-confidence. Why are we like that? Why do we put up with it? Can we change it? The short answer is yes, we can change our behaviour. We can change our attitude and outlook. Changing behaviour is an internal concept which is exhibited externally. How badly do you want to change? And what are you prepared to do to make that change?

Most people think that they cannot alter their behaviour. This is not the case. We are all, to a greater or lesser degree, conditioned to behave in a certain way, this is due to a number of factors. Some of these factors are social, hereditary, economic, cultural and environmental. Any one or a combination can/will have an influence on your behaviour. But that does not mean that you cannot change, alter or adapt your behaviour. You don't always have to accept things as they are, as though they were set in stone. You have within you the abilities and skills not only to stand up for yourself – but to change. You can change how you think, feel and act.

CASE STUDY

At school I was considered to be a bit backward and there was a case made for putting me back a year. I was kept on by my teacher, Miss Hunter, who showed great faith in me. Her class size was a massive 48! However, my experience at secondary school was not great. For three years in a row, I failed all my Standard Grades and eventually left school with no qualifications.

After I left school, I was working in a dead-end job in a dead-end housing scheme. But when I was 18, I decided to change my behaviour and made two decisions which drastically altered my life. First, I decided to go to evening classes at a Further Education College and, second, I joined Shettleston Harriers Athletic Club. Working at my evening classes, I eventually achieved the necessary Standard and Higher Grades for entry into university. And by joining Shettleston Harriers, I overcame chronic asthma, from which I had suffered since the age of seven, and eventually ran a marathon in 2hrs 25mins.

By changing my behaviour and my way of thinking, I overcame all those negative put-downs and comments from which I had suffered for so many years. It proved to me that I could change my behaviour and achieve things!

Shouting for your Self to be heard does not involve running up on top of a hill and shouting! It is that deep, burning desire to be who you want to be that needs to be heard. Often we store up resentment of things that could have been or might have been, only to find that all we have left is disappointment and anxiety. Don't settle for that sombre attitude that nothing can be altered and that your life is just an existence.

- Decide today to make changes in your life.
- Stand up and let your Self be heard.
- Don't be like a volcano that occasionally erupts then reverts back to making rumbling noises of complaint, unfairness and 'poor me' syndrome.

All of us have an inner-voice. Some people refer to it as their conscience, others give it different names. It doesn't really matter what you call it, so long as you can recognise it and control it. You can't and mustn't ignore it.

- Don't be afraid to listen to the sound of your own inner-voice.
- Let it speak loudly and positively to you.
- Remember that it is unique to you.
- Use it wisely to help you make those simple changes to your life that will have a huge impact.
- Let your inner-voice be strong and loud.
- Let it be heard.

Let your inner-voice be sensible and lead you into making sound decisions that will affect your life. For example, if you have led a sedentary lifestyle for many years and your inner-voice tells you that it's time to do something about your lack of exercise, it is hard to ignore – especially if that voice is strong and loud.

The problem arises when we have not fully listened and gone headlong into a rigorous fitness regime. Our inner-voice would have urged caution and our response should have been to take it slowly. If you can walk for five minutes without being breathless – then walk for five minutes. It's five minutes of exercise that you did not do before. There is no point in trying to do 30–45 minutes exercise three times a week when you are clearly not ready for it.

CASE STUDY

A young woman came to see me to ask for help in her attempt to give up smoking. She had tried all sorts of remedies, from patches to hypnosis, and all points in between. After a long and wide-ranging discussion about her craving for cigarettes, we decided on a plan that might help her. With any approach, there is no guarantee that it will work. But as all of us are unique and different, it was important that a solution or plan was acceptable to her and met her individual needs.

We settled on a 20 week programme! Now, if you're a smoker, this might sound daunting but in actual fact it was quite simplistic in its approach.

Each morning she would buy a packet of 20 cigarettes. On the first Monday of the programme, she bought her packet then took out one cigarette and 'ceremoniously' put it in a bin. Every day that week, she did the same thing, thereby only smoking 19 cigarettes a day. What we were attempting to do was to quieten the inner-voice of craving and substitute it with other 'positive voices' of change. By reducing her number of cigarettes – by one at a time – week by week, she eventually reached the stage (after 19 weeks) when she bought her packet of 20 and threw 19 cigarettes in the bin. This then left her with only one cigarette to smoke. Although this was an expensive way to give up smoking, for her it was money well spent. And she supplemented her positive efforts in those 20 weeks by joining a keep-fit class and altering her diet.

We not only have to listen to our inner-voice, we must also learn to control it. Otherwise we could make the wrong decisions. Your inner-voice may tell you that you need to lose weight. With the inexorable rise in obesity, there is a sense of fear and alarm regarding people's weight. Your inner-voice may advocate a crash diet, but this has to be avoided. By taking control of your dietary intake, you will be in a much better position to control your weight than by going on a crash diet. The point here is that there may be some conflict between what you want to do and what your inner-voice is telling you to do.

For the vast majority of people, accelerated fasting and food deprivation are dangerous routes to take to losing weight. It is more appropriate and longer lasting if you start to make small adjustments to your lifestyle. Remember a diet should not be for life, but changes to your lifestyle are. Doing things in small ways can ensure a more permanent change takes place, rather than the many quick-fix solutions often highlighted in the media.

So learn to stand up for your Self. Learn to shout for your Self. Begin by taking a closer interest in your own physical and mental wellbeing. Turn away from those negative thoughts that you have and replace them with shouts of joy and change. By making just a small alteration to your daily routine or lifestyle, you will immediately act and feel a different person. You will be more at ease with yourself and your life will be more enriched by making those changes.

A lifetime of change is guaranteed. But what is not guaranteed is the quality of those changes. Only you can determine that. A lot will be determined by how much you want to embrace, accept, adapt to those changes. Nothing remains the same. Nothing remains static. Change is inevitable so we all have choices to make. You can shout: I want to change the way I feel, the way I act, the way I think, dress, behave. Whatever it is you want to change, you have to shout for it. If you don't, you resign yourself to a life of ifs, buts and maybes.

Choosing to do nothing is the easy option. But if, deep down, you want to fundamentally change your lifestyle, follow the words of the song Lulu made famous in the 1960s – and SHOUT!

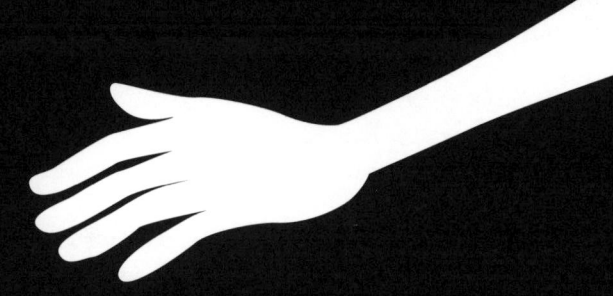

Chapter Nine

The Quiet Self

In the modern world of 24/7 and instant communication, it is hard for people to find the time to relax, reflect or even think about their lives. Everybody seems to be in a hurry. Everybody seems to have less time for talking or meeting people. We seem to have less time for ourselves.

Instant messages and texts have replaced the need to actually *talk* to someone. We seem to be avoiding all physical contact with each other, and have become the 'invisible' society. Yet somehow the need to be on our own, with our own thoughts, is even greater.

The Five Minute Rule is something you should seriously consider. The basic premise is simple: take just five minutes of your time, at some point in the day, to just stop what you are doing and think or reflect.

That's all there is to it. What you think or reflect on is entirely up to you. All you have to do is switch off your iPod, mobile phone, TV or computer, and let your mind wander.

It's not new. The need for a quiet and contemplative period in our lives has always been there. Whatever historical period you care to read about, you find that people took time out to reflect and think on things. Although it was primarily the function of monks and learned people, it has always been an important aspect of life. Yet we don't do it often enough.

We have lost the art of reflection and how to enjoy the quietness and stillness of life. Somehow the idea does not fit well into the modern lifestyle, but nothing could be further from the truth. Why is it that so many tourists, while visiting great cathedrals, monasteries and other places of worship, stop and sit for a few moments alone with their thoughts? Much more is going on than just admiring the architecture. They are spending time with their Quiet Self. Unfortunately they don't carry on with this concept when they get back home, and it becomes a faded memory in a holiday photograph. But you don't have to go to a cathedral or a place of worship to be with your Quiet Self. It can be done anywhere – even in your own home. The main point is to find the time and space for it.

Can you imagine sitting at home listening to nothing but the sound of your own heartbeat? Try it. Start with five minutes today. Put yourself into a relaxing position and let your mind drift away. Don't worry if you fall asleep – it probably means that you needed it anyway! If you start to do this daily, you may find that eventually you are able to relax better and you will feel refreshed afterwards.

CASE STUDY

Kate Pace, world champion in downhill skiing, told Jeff Grout and Sarah Perrin in their book *Mind Games*: 'I think the most important thing is always looking for that quiet time when you can sit back, be by yourself, relax and simply be quiet. Sometimes you feel you are constantly running all the time. You never get that quiet time. That time was very important to me because it pulled me away from my sport and gave me the opportunity to really sit back and think. I don't think I could have achieved those big wins if I hadn't had that quiet time to stop and think. Now I have to schedule that quiet time. I need to sit alone and reflect.'

Take some time out of your busy day for Your Self. Letting go helps to regenerate your mind and body. All too often we allow ourselves to get caught up in the maelstrom of modern living, without really appreciating who and what we are. Self-reflection allows you to think about those issues a little bit more deeply.

The Quiet Self allows you to bring your mind and body into a better state of equilibrium. Just five minutes each day is not a lot to ask. It is not some mystical or metaphysical existentialist phenomenon that you're being asked to undertake!

Your Quiet Self is just as important to develop as any other part of your other selves. It has to be nurtured, fed, looked after and massaged. It has to be continually used. Get into the habit of doing this and the habit will get into you.

Being quiet and still are strange concepts in Western societies and cultures. Yet many thousands of people in China, Japan, Tibet and other countries, practise devoting time and space for themselves in very public places. They have done this for many centuries because they realise the importance of the alignment of the body and the mind. They 'listen' to their bodies and minds.

There are a plethora of programmes, based on Eastern culture, which you can choose from. Most are a variation of the one theme, the Self. Transcendental Meditation (TM), Yoga, Tai Chi, Progressive Muscle Relaxation (PMR) and others, all carry roughly the same message about looking after the body's physical and spiritual wellbeing.

Unfortunately we in the West do not have the same deep spiritual level or tradition, and have a reluctance to embrace alternative ideas and theories. However, the most important point is not whether one method is better than another, but the principle behind them all.

If you find the idea of participating in an organised class a bit off-putting, you can still follow this practice at home on your own. It's not rocket science.

- Sit in your armchair and let your mind and body relax for five minutes.
- There is no great mystique about sitting quietly on your own with your own thoughts. Many people do so in a place of worship – your home is no different.
- There are no prescriptive feelings or sensations that you should have or experience.
- There is no right or wrong way to do it – just do it!
- Believe that it can bring some calmness and order into your otherwise chaotic life.
- Giving your Quiet Self some quality time may help you find that elusive peace of mind – a valuable asset in today's frantic world.

But what should you think about? That's up to you. You might just want to sit and listen to some reflective music, read a book, or just close your eyes and let your mind drift. You may have something specific that you want to think about – perhaps a major decision that you have to make. It really doesn't matter what you do with your five minutes. There is no right or wrong approach.

CASE STUDY

Footballing legend George Best:

The night before every game, George Best would spend 5–10 minutes going over in his mind what he was going to do in the match.

At a press conference before an International between Northern Ireland and Holland, a journalist asked him what he was going to do in the game. Best said that as soon as the whistle blew and he got the ball he would run and nutmeg the Dutch legend, Johann Cruyff. The assembled press laughed. That night George replayed in his mind what he was going to do. The following evening, as soon as the game started and Best received the ball, he went straight for Johann Cruyff and nutmegged him – much to the delight of the crowd. He also gave an inverted Churchillian sign to the press box!

Many famous people have used quiet moments to contemplate issues facing them. Don't you think Michelangelo would have taken some time out to reflect on his great masterpieces, or Beethoven when composing his wonderful symphonies? In the literary world of creative writing, did Tolstoy not need many breaks when he was writing *War and Peace*? What about Steinbeck when writing *The Grapes of Wrath*, or more recently J.K. Rowling sitting in an Edinburgh café writing her famous Harry Potter books?

Just think for a moment about all the great inventions over the last 100 years. If Edison had not stopped to reflect on his experiments, the chances are that he would never have invented the light bulb. Despite some 10,000 attempts, he kept going and was eventually successful. If Marconi had not assessed his invention at every stage, would he have invented the radio? If it's good enough for them, it is surely good enough for you.

Taking quiet time just for our Selves doesn't mean that we have to cut ourselves off from society. Instead, cherish the moments when your mind is free and you have peace to be with your own thoughts. This is not some mumbo-jumbo. It is not some mystical meditation involving incense, or some incoherent chanting. It is simply:

- to enjoy the sense of peace and quiet
- to get back in touch with yourself
- to re-charge your mind and body
- to take care of your mental, physical and spiritual health and wellbeing
- your Quiet Self demanding that you give it time and attention

Use this special time to find out more about yourself and what you can achieve.

- Use your time wisely.
- Live each day to the fullest.
- Don't short-change yourself by thinking that you do not need any form of quiet time.
- Ignoring your Quiet Self carries a heavy price.
- Do not ignore the five minute rule.

Recent research has discovered that some form of reflection or meditation can reduce pain perception, relieve psychological distress and increase volume in specific areas of the brain. It has also been associated with enhanced activity in the areas of the brain involved in attention, perception, memory and empathy. Your mind is an untapped source of imagination, creativity, problem-solving, forward-thinking and much more. So don't lose it – use it!

- Be still.
- Be quiet.
- Take 5!

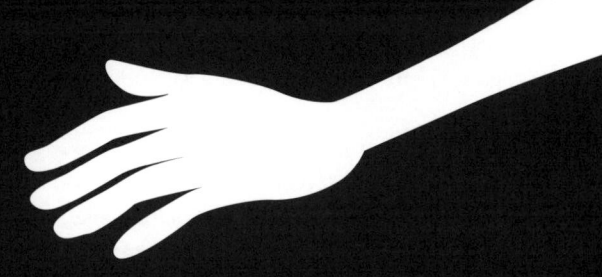

Chapter Ten

The 10% Rule

In addition to finding some quiet time, we also need to find time for our creative side – whatever that may be. And that's where the 10% Rule comes in.

Basically the 10% rule is designed to encourage you to spend 10% of your day/week on something that pleases you – something that gives you enjoyment, pleasure and satisfaction.

Irrespective of who you are or what you do, finding 10% of the day to do something that pleases only YOU is essential. Too often we allow ourselves to feel guilty about wasting time on so-called frivolities. We feel that we should be doing something more 'productive' like housework, or working at home. But this feeling of guilt has to change or you will face burnout or a breakdown.

You should never feel guilty about finding time for yourself. There is tremendous pressure to conform to society's demands, work demands or relationship demands. The trick is to balance all of them equally and to designate that time which is just for you.

10% of your day only amounts to between 1–2 hours. Yet that time is important for you to pursue and do something that gives you pleasure. It could be piano lessons, going to art classes, attending a keep-fit class, or writing that book you never managed to start. But it is doing something that makes you happy.

The moment you step into a taxi the driver switches on the meter and it starts ticking. It's the same with your life! The meter of life is already running and clocking up the days, weeks and years and the question you have to ask yourself is: What have I done with all that time? You can't turn the meter back, but it's not too late to put a little self-enjoyment back into your life. Explore your creative side and see how far you go with it. Do a little bit each day – find your 10%.

CASE STUDY

A man named Spencer Silver was working in the 3M research labs in 1970, trying to find a strong adhesive. He developed a new adhesive but it was too weak. However, he did not discard it. In 1974 another 3M scientist, Arthur Fry, was singing in the church choir. He used markers to keep his place in the hymnal, but they kept falling out of the book. Remembering Silver's adhesive, Fry experimented with it and found that the markers stayed in place, yet lifted off without damaging the pages. They are now famously called 3M Post-it notes. If Fry had not taken the 10% of his time to work on Silver's adhesive, then Post-it notes would not have seen the light of day.

Make the 10% a commitment to yourself – a commitment for you to do something that is just for YOU and nobody else. We spend so much time doing things for other people – we work for them, care for them, serve them… and we forget about ourselves.

Some people will consider us selfish if we take time to do things just for ourselves. But why? There is nothing wrong in being a bit SELFish! No matter what age we are, we can and should find time to 'challenge' ourselves to achieve things.

When that light of inspiration and freedom of thought is dimmed, the light in our creative lives begins to close over and eventually any creativity that we once had is gone. Once you allow yourself to be a prisoner of inactivity, you are at the mercy of reality TV, reality conversation and a reality lifestyle. You become a slave to a spoon-fed, myopic, surreal and fantasy world.

- Life is for learning and challenging ourselves.
- Age is no precursor or barrier to imagination and creativity.
- Become passionate about the 10% rule, before the 90% rule devours you into a life of boredom and futility.
- Challenge yourself to change some of those dull habits you have acquired.
- Throw off the cobwebs that have trapped and snared you into a life of drudgery and monotony.

Why not start now? Put this book down and go and do something you have always wanted to do. Start your 10% rule now and come back when you have done it.

How does it feel? Strange? Uncomfortable? Did you have a guilty conscience? Did you feel you should be doing something 'more meaningful'? Did the world come to an end? Now that you have done it once and broken the mould – the taboo – it won't be so hard to do the next time. Each day provides an opportunity for you to start and to continue on that project, book, new skill, or whatever it is you want to achieve. All too often people give up too early because the going gets tough. Your obstacles in life are there to be overcome – if you want to. If Edison had not taken the 10% of time that he needed to invent the light bulb and persevered for over 10,000 attempts, we might be still living in the dark!

Remember the biggest obstacle to you implementing the 10% Rule is – YOU. The main objective is for you to find the time, space and the discipline to promote your own personal development. We all have dreams, desires, goals and things that we want to do and achieve.

Life is not a dress rehearsal. You only have one chance at it, so make the most of it – chase that dream and take the 10% time you need to start to pursue that goal.

CASE STUDY

John Grisham was working some 60–70 hours a week as a lawyer. One day he overheard a harrowing case in the courthouse and was inspired to write a novel. He started getting up at 5am every day to get in several hours of writing before he went to work. In the end he spent three years writing his book, *A Time To Kill*, which went on to be the first of his many bestsellers. He used the 10% Rule to succeed!

Before you go to sleep, or before you even get out of bed in the morning, try to plan your day and programme in when you are going to take that 10% time just for you. Finding time is not easy, especially for mothers who have to balance a work and home life. But for people – like them – living with stress, it should be a priority!

There is no time limit on the 10% Rule; it can be anything from 30 minutes to two hours. Just make sure you stick to the principle and find the time. You'll be amazed at how much happier and fulfilled you will feel. Sometimes we convince ourselves that we are far too busy to take time out; that we are indispensable at work, that our valuable time is too precious to waste on frivolities like hobbies. You couldn't be more wrong!

- You are not indispensable.
- Spending some 'quality' time on your Self is never wasted and is important for your own personal development.
- Never be afraid to pursue the things that You enjoy.
- Stop feeling guilty every time you are doing something for you.

The 10% Rule is a guide on how to start doing some of the things you have been putting off for too long. Remember: yesterday has gone, tomorrow is still to come, today is all you have. So spend some of the time on your Self!

Your personal space, development and growth are just as important as anybody else's. Find your 10% and watch how you begin to feel more at ease with yourself, more balanced and more in harmony with other parts of your life.

Don't let time run away from you. Take control of your life. Don't leave any regrets on that blank canvas, that unwritten book, that unfinished music lesson, that abandoned PC course, that foreign language you wanted to learn, that hill-walking group you joined.

Whatever it is that you've always wanted to achieve, go and find that 10% time you need. Then watch the change in YOU, the transformation in your life.

10% time on your Self = 90% Happiness!

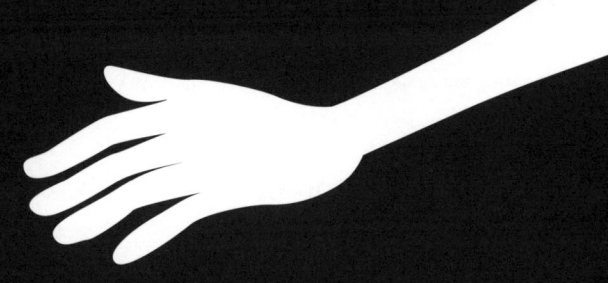

Chapter Eleven

The Selfish Self

Do you consider yourself to be a selfish person? Do you put yourself first before anyone or anything else? Most of us would say no, but in this chapter you are invited to be SELFISH!

This part of your make-up may make you feel uneasy, as it goes against most people's principles to be seen as selfish. But what I'm proposing is that you have to be a little bit selfish to look after your Self.

You need to be selfish about making sure your needs are met, specifically when it comes to looking after your physical and mental wellbeing. It is important that you take the necessary time out to look after your own needs.

Meeting the demands of everyday life can be a struggle. It is also a juggling act between home, family and work. Each of these components requires your time and attention, so it's hard sometimes to keep a balance and give equal time and attention to all of them.

The danger is that you can be overwhelmed, which can lead to burnout, exhaustion and stress. Some of the physical signs of burnout are increased heart rate, an increase in sleep loss, being more susceptible to colds/flu and infections, a decrease in appetite and an increase in fatigue. Some of the psychological factors in burnout are more bad moods, increased mental exhaustion, a decrease in self-esteem and feeling stressed on a daily basis.

There are three easy ways to address these issues and to identify when things are getting too much for you. First, there is your sense of self-awareness. You have to try to recognise that you are suffering from some form of stress/anxiety and seek medical advice. Second, take some time out from whatever is causing you distress, anxiety and fatigue. If the symptoms are identified early enough, you might be able to deal with the situation yourself by taking some time out. Third, it may be that some form of relaxation technique is what you require as a means of coping with the trials and tribulations of everyday life.

There are many ways of dealing with the stresses and strains of everyday life and it's up to you to find which method suits you. Sometimes just talking to a good friend is as good a way as any to deal with those issues that you find troublesome. Being selfish can help prevent things from happening to you in the future and help you to cope with them better.

Remember: prevention is better than cure!

CASE STUDY

A client came to see me about changing his chaotic and hectic lifestyle. He was a high-flyer in a large multi-national company and felt that he was constantly under pressure to be successful. There was a severe strain on his family life as he worked late most evenings and had little or no time left for himself or his family. By the time he got home his two little girls were always asleep.

He felt lethargic and lacking in energy. Although he had previously kept active, the pressure of work now prevented him from maintaining a keep-fit regime. As well as working late, he also had a tendency to work at weekends, thus adding more stress.

Through our discussions, it became clear that he had no ability to 'delegate' tasks and responsibilities to others. In addition, his poor time-management meant that he was always rushing to and from meetings, either snatching a sandwich on the go or sitting down to heavy business lunches. This had caused an unhealthy increase in his weight.

After several meetings, it was agreed that he had to become a bit more 'SELFish'. The idea was that if he did not look after himself, how was he going to look after others?

One of the first things we agreed on was the introduction of a weekly plan that would allocate times for exercise, family, lunch breaks, etc. These times and activities were to be – as far as possible – sacrosanct. For example, at least three times a week, he would have to go for a walk at lunchtime.

Over a period of time he learned how to delegate with responsibility and his time-management skills improved. He also found time for HIMSELF. He dramatically reduced the amount of work he took home and stopped working at the weekends altogether. The net result was a dramatic improvement in the quality of his life. By changing his work patterns and being a bit more SELFish, he gradually reduced his workload. And by finding valuable time for himself, he managed to turn his – and his family's – life around.

We can find it difficult to spend some time on ourselves, feeling embarrassed about doing something for our own enjoyment.

- Don't be embarrassed or ashamed.
- You have a right to do something which pleases only you.

- Every day you should find something that gives you pleasure.
- Many people like to jog, walk or keep fit as it gives them a sense of achievement.
- Make space and time to be on your own, sometimes to think things through or just recharge your batteries.
- You are not abdicating your responsibilities by doing something for yourself – instead you are better prepared to face them.
- Looking after yourself is paramount to your overall wellbeing.
- Don't wait until you feel under pressure or stressed out – find the time that you need to relax and rest.

Think about the D.I.Y. approach to looking after yourself. This concept is based on the common sense psychology that the answer for most of us lies at the end of our fingertips. That's where you'll find the telephone directory that contains information on classes, courses, self-help programmes – even friends.

Remember that your needs are just as important as anyone else's, so you owe it to yourself to be selfish to improve the quality of your life, resolve conflicts better and solve problems. You win no heroic medals for putting yourself into a situation of acute stress or anxiety, whether at work, at home, or in a relationship.

The importance of quality time for yourself cannot be underestimated. Too often people give up on things because of 'external' pressure or because of the demands placed on them. They lose out on their own development as a person and their own happiness and self-worth. Don't let this happen to you. Do not fall into that trap.

If you enjoy going for a swim, walking, jogging or any other activity, then you must keep it going. Why should you stop going or doing what pleases you? Your continuous development as a person does not stop at a certain point in your life – it continues. No matter what changes take place around you or to you – be it work, home, family or relationships – your personal development has to continue. So being selfish is not to be frowned upon.

Many top people make it to the height of their profession, in sport or in business, by being selfish and single-minded. Many of them have made great personal sacrifices and denied themselves an easier lifestyle, because being selfish was a necessary ingredient for their success.

CASE STUDY

Ellen MacArthur, the world-famous yachtswoman, made personal sacrifices to achieve her ambition. In Jeff Grout and Sarah Perrin's book *Mind Games* she explains: 'When I was about 14, I was already trying to save up my money to buy a small boat.

> My first boat was an eight-foot dinghy. I had been saving up since the age of eight. Saving for a boat was a massive goal, which is why for lunch at school I'd either have nothing, or soup which cost four pence from the soup machine, or mashed potato and baked beans which cost a total of eight pence. I saved everything because we did not get pocket money as kids, and birthdays and Christmases were quite spaced out, so it was basically about making savings every day.'
>
> She went on to become the fastest woman and the youngest person to circumnavigate the earth in a single-handed yacht race.

Although you may not have to be as single-minded as some, you do have to think about what you need as a person. You have to ask yourself:

- How selfish do I want/need to be?
- How much does it matter to me if I am a bit more selfish?
- Will people think less of me because I take time out to look after myself?

We all have a selfish gene, but most of us keep it subdued or suppressed. We were taught as children that being selfish was bad, so we frown upon those who display that kind of streak. But this is a barrier that you have to put into context.

Just because you think about yourself does not mean that you have abandoned all your principles and values. Far from it! If all the great writers, musicians and inventors were 'selfish' in taking some time out to look after their wellbeing, why can't you?

- What makes you so different that you don't appear to need time to be yourself?
- Why can't you take some quality time for yourself?
- Why don't you do something today that will please you?
- What is holding you back?
- Are you using the old excuse that you're too busy and that people depend on you?
- Are you waiting for someone to say to you that it's alright to take some time for yourself?

If the answer to the final question is 'yes', you'll have a long wait because nobody is going to tell you. You have to start today – right now – yourself.

Your journey through life has to include taking time just for you. Taking care of yourself is your responsibility – don't neglect it. How can you expect to look after somebody else when you can't look after yourself?

Try the 'Selfish Questionnaire':

1) I never think of others before myself.   Y/N

2) I never leave the last sweet/biscuit for someone else.   Y/N

3) I never fit my life around other people.   Y/N

4) I don't expect to do things for myself.   Y/N

5) I think I deserve special treatment.   Y/N

6) I get upset when people call me 'selfish'.   Y/N

7) I always get my own way.   Y/N

8) I hate it when I do not get my own way.   Y/N

9) I always put myself first.   Y/N

10) I never think of others.   Y/N

If you have answered 'Yes' to any of the questions, then you are selfish! Don't worry – it's not a crime. In essence there are no right or wrong answers to the questionnaire – it all comes down to your perception of yourself. In some ways the world is a much more self-centred place nowadays, and the opportunities to be totally selfish are vast.

You may have to work hard at being selfish. It may not be easy for you. But it is important for your own personal development and growth.

- You neglect your Self at your peril.
- Never underestimate the needs that you have.
- Never put off what you want to do and use lame excuses for not being selfish.
- Life is a challenge – if you don't rise to it, you will fall short of your dreams, desires and goals.
- We all have a purpose in life – only you know what yours is, and you must find out how to get there.
- It's the journey through life that counts, not just the destination.
- Be persistent with yourself – don't give up.
- Don't sell yourself short by thinking that you are unimportant.

Your importance to many people will depend largely on how well you look after yourself. So make a commitment that each day you will do something to enhance your wellbeing. Make a determined effort to take the time to get rid of those negative fears that prevent you from being who you are and who you want to be.

Think about how you feel about yourself, how you 'look'. Think about how you affect other people. Think about how confident you are. Think about those things that you want to do, to achieve. Think about the time for you to be 'SELFish'!

The quest for a balanced lifestyle is the aim of many people. Unfortunately too many fall into the trap of tilting that balance to the detriment of their own self-worth, self-esteem and, ultimately, their self-confidence. They let themselves down by underachieving, by settling for second best, or giving up on themselves.

Yet you owe it to yourself – and those around you – to be the person you always wanted to be. The only obstacles are those that you choose to recognise. What is stopping you from making a start? What is preventing you from using and developing those skills or talents that you have? Maybe you're afraid of what you might find out about yourself. Or are you afraid of failure? Are you giving up on those dreams and goals that once shone brightly in your mind? Do you feel that your life is settled so it's too late to start?

Nobody is asking you to make grand, dramatic changes to your life. Just give some time to Your Self – you deserve it!

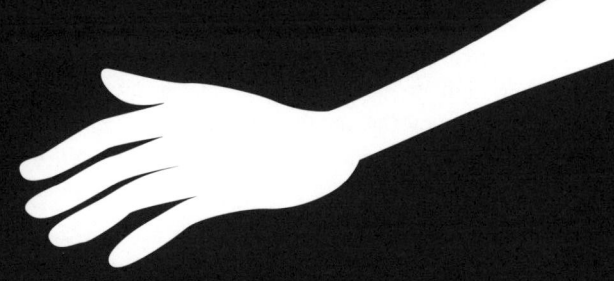

Chapter Twelve

The Great Self-Believers

All of us have met, read or heard about people who are great Self-Believers. They usually have certain traits or characteristics in common and exude a confidence which sometimes borders on arrogance. They usually have plenty to say for themselves too!

Many of them display a sense of vanity, which can put people off them but make others extremely envious. The question is: how did they get this great self-belief? Were they born with it? What makes them have a greater self-belief than you and me? Is it genetic? Environmental? Their upbringing? Or is it a great deal of self-determination?

It may be a combination, instead of any one single event. Perhaps what we should be asking is if any of them ever displayed or showed periods of self-doubt? And, if they did, how did they overcome that?

For some great self-believers, having periods of self-doubt is a good thing because it allows them to question their motives, desire, commitment, motivation and dedication. They use that time to reflect on their goals and purpose in life. On the other hand, some have always displayed a single-minded approach and appear never to have experienced a sense of self-doubt. Instead, their commitment and determination in the pursuit of a particular course, objective, idea or challenge, has been the dominant factor in their lives.

Having a great deal of self-belief is an important characteristic in the personal make-up of many successful people. All of them – whether in sport, business or any other walk of life – have experienced the pain of setbacks and disappointment. Very few people have found the road to success to be completely straightforward.

You have to ask yourself: just how strong is my self-belief? Is it strong enough to allow me to rise and conquer periods of self-doubt, lack of self-confidence and low self-esteem?

- Self-belief cannot be given to you.
- You have to find a way to develop it yourself.
- You have to have something that you really want to do or achieve.
- You must want this badly enough for you to pursue it.
- You must start to really believe that you can achieve it.

Self-belief can come to you slowly, if you let it. All you have to do is to keep working at it and, bit by bit, you will get better. It will not be an overnight success.

Make a small start by looking at yourself in the mirror. This may seem uncomfortable or strange at first, but keep reminding yourself that you are a unique individual with your own talents and skills. You are a valued human being with a lot to offer. By repeating this over and over again to yourself, you will soon begin to accept it and your self-belief will gradually improve.

You should do this every morning. Looking in the mirror at yourself is not conceited or arrogant – it's the opposite. We are what we see, so this is a reaffirmation of your worth. In the mirror you will find the biggest obstacle to your lack of self-belief and self-confidence – YOU!

Yes, you are the biggest obstacle that you have to overcome in order to achieve a greater sense of self-belief. If you can overcome 'yourself' each day, then you have a chance of being successful. A lack of self-belief is a mind-set that you have got yourself into. And if you have a limited amount of self-belief, then you will have a limited amount of desire to improve to succeed.

So who are the great Self-Believers in life? They are all around us. People like Sir Alex Ferguson, Lord Alan Sugar, Sir Chris Hoy, Daley Thomson, Cristiano Ronaldo, Jose Mourinho, Sir Nick Faldo, Andy Murray, Roger Federer, Dame Kelly Holmes, Sir Richard Branson and Duncan Bannatyne. The list is endless. And they all seem to have something in common – a desire, a commitment and an unshakeable belief in themselves and in what they wanted to achieve.

Far too many of us have had self-belief knocked out of us at an early age. We were told that we were not good enough, tall enough or smart enough, to achieve something. How many people have you known who have shown potential, only for it to be snatched away from them? How often have you heard that you need to lower your expectations, because you're aiming too high? The world is full of people who will try to dampen your enthusiasm instead of raising your spirits. Some of the successful people mentioned were put down when they were younger and discouraged from achieving great things. Yet somehow, despite all the setbacks and disappointments, they persevered and ultimately came through.

Take the story of Thomas Edison, the inventor of the light bulb – an everyday item we all take for granted. It took Edison 10,000 attempts before he was successful and discovered a way to produce the light bulb. When he was asked why he did not give up and why it took so many unsuccessful attempts, Edison replied that he had 'found 10,000 ways not to invent the light bulb'!

When we talk about the great Self-Believers, the example of Albert Einstein is a salutary reminder never to label people too early in life. Einstein could not read until he was seven years of age. He was rejected by many colleges. He was considered backward in school and yet he became one of the greatest minds in history.

The author John Grisham would rise at 5am every morning to write. When he completed his first book he sent it to a publisher, but the book was not selling very well and Grisham took it back. He began to sell it himself and the rest, as they say, is history.

Age is no barrier to having great self-belief. The founder of KFC worked on the railways for 46 years and visited over 500 restaurants before his original recipe was finally accepted.
And perhaps one of the greatest examples of having great self-belief and inner-strength was Wilma Rudolph. Wilma was 20th of 22 children. She was very ill as a child, having contracted polio and scarlet fever, and was forced to wear a leg brace to strengthen her leg. By the age of 13 Wilma had developed a 'rhythmic' walk. She then decided that she wanted to be a runner.

Encouraged by her mother, she took off her leg brace and began to run. For the next two years she finished last in every race that she entered. Eventually she won a race, and then another. For the next few years every race that she entered she won and this little girl, who was told she would never walk again, went on to win three Olympic Gold Medals. Courage, determination and, above all else, a great sense of self-belief – that is what Wilma had.

Another example of overcoming adversity is the story of Bethany Hamilton. Bethany was 14 years of age and a highly successful surfer, who had won many championships. She was competing in Hawaii when she was attacked by a shark. The shark overturned her surfboard and ripped off her arm. Bethany was frantically trying to attract the attention of the crowd on the beach, but they initially thought she was waving at them. Eventually she managed to get to the shore, where she passed out, and was rushed to hospital. Some six weeks after this terrible accident, Bethany was back surfing and finished fourth in a major championship.

Sir Roger Bannister was the first athlete to break the four-minute mile. Up until that point, many distinguished medical professionals, physiologists and coaches believed it was not physically possible for anyone to run a mile in under four minutes. In 1954 Roger Bannister ran one mile in 3 mins 59 secs on the track at Iffley Road, Oxford. And within a matter of days, six more athletes had broken the four-minute mile barrier. Bannister overcame all the doubters and showed great determination and self-belief for others to follow.

The late Sir Edmund Hillary and Sherpa Tenzing became the first men to climb Mount Everest without the aid of oxygen – a feat considered physically impossible at the time.

Our world is full of people who have overcome tremendous odds with a great deal of self-belief. In every walk of life people have overcome the setbacks and disappointments that life has thrown at them. All of them have a great sense of who they are and what they want to achieve. They all have an unwavering belief in themselves, a desire and commitment.

Where and how strong is your self-belief? Did you give up too early because the going got tough? Did you not have the mental strength to recover from setbacks and disappointments? Where is your commitment and determination?

Just think what the world would be like if all the modern inventors had given up because the going got tough. Imagine a world without TV if J. L. Baird had decided to give up, or what if Marconi had decided that inventing the radio was more trouble than it was worth? If Alexander Graham Bell had decided to abandon his telephone invention, because he was frustrated at not making a breakthrough after so many attempts, you probably wouldn't have a mobile phone today.

We sometimes fail to appreciate the struggle and personal sacrifice so many people have had to make to achieve their ambitions. All successful people have failed at one time or another. What they have though, is a capacity to learn from mistakes, failure and setbacks. They remain undeterred and have a great capacity to push themselves and to never give in. Can this be said of you?

- Do you give in at the slightest disappointment?
- Are you less determined when things go wrong?
- Are you a defeatist?
- Do you mentally tell yourself that your failure was not your fault?
- Do you convince yourself that you don't have the necessary skills or talent to succeed?
- Do you think that your self-belief is not as strong as other people's?

If you answered 'yes', it's about time that you changed your thinking. Start thinking positively instead of negatively. This is easier said than done, which is why there are so many training courses available on assertiveness, self-confidence, self-esteem, etc.

We allow ourselves to be convinced that we are not as good as somebody else. But it's not too late. Stop reading now, and write down the things that you are good at.

You may surprise yourself at what is on your list. Look! You are not so useless after all. You must look at what you want to achieve out of life, not what you don't want to achieve. If you are good at something, become better at it. If you have a talent or skill for something, nurture it. Don't waste what you have!

CASE STUDY

Olympic gold medallist John Naber, 100m backstroke, 1976

John Naber was at home, lying on the floor watching the 1972 Olympics, and saw swimmer Mark Spitz win seven gold medals.

A backstroke swimmer himself, Naber was inspired by Spitz's efforts. Then he watched Roland Matthes win the 100m backstroke in 56.3 seconds.

Naber's Personal Best was 59.5secs for the same distance. He considered that 55.5 would win the gold medal in four years' time, which meant he was four seconds off the pace but had four years to improve his Personal Best. He then broke the four years down into one second a year, and calculated that this would mean improving by 1/10th of a second a month: 1/300th of a second a day. So he trained from 6–8am every morning and from 4–6pm every evening, six days a week. This meant reducing his time by 1/200th of a second every hour. He even calculated that from the time his eyelids started to close until the time they actually touched, 5/1200th of a second had elapsed.

Naber went on to win the gold medal. He did it by getting the most out of what talent he had.

Your personal development and progress as a human being will ultimately depend on how much time, energy, effort and commitment you are prepared to put into your life. Your sense of achievement will increase once you release yourself and start to believe in yourself a bit more.

Tiger Woods is undoubtedly the finest golfer of his generation, yet there is an assumption that he has never been beaten and is 'invincible'. In fact, when he was younger, Tiger was beaten more than once and even now he is unsuccessful on occasions.

Muhammad Ali was the same. His 'invincibility' came after he had recovered and learned from previous losses and setbacks.

If you look at all the great sportsmen and women, you will find that at some point in their lives they have suffered defeat. Some have even recovered from serious, career-threatening injuries. Yet they all had that same drive and hunger to push themselves to reach the top of their sport.

Take a moment to reflect on those athletes who competed at the recent Paralympic Games in Beijing. Think of all the physical and mental barriers they must have had to endure. All of them should be a source of inspiration to us. It would have been easy for many of them to give up – but they didn't.

What they have in common is the same self-belief that you have. The only difference is that they have held on to theirs – what about YOU? They also possess a strong mental approach, which can be highlighted by the following attributes:

1) Commitment

2) Desire

3) Focus

4) Confidence

5) Self-belief

6) Positive outlook

Not all of us have all these characteristics – some of us will have more of one characteristic than others. But if there is no self-belief, then there is every likelihood that the rest will not follow.

If you feel that you lack some of these characteristics and that you have a low self-belief, don't worry. We gain more self-belief when we feel we have 'mastered' a skill or technique. Remember that feeling you had when you first managed to ride a bike unaided, or passed your driving test?

If you feel that you are lacking in certain skills, just go back to the feeling you had when you mastered your last skill and put the same approach into effect. The great self-believers are, in a sense, no different from you and me. They have experienced periods of doubt, but it is their strong sense of self-belief that separates them from the rest of us. They work at their self-belief while too many of us let ours wither on the vine.

You can start to develop your own self-belief by repeating over and over again, 'I CAN and I WILL.' If you keep repeating this to yourself, eventually you will come to *believe* it. And once you *really* believe in yourself, the next part is to act on your self-belief. Take inspiration from whatever source you can find and develop your own mental strength, continually reminding yourself of those successes you have had in the past.

Developing a more sustained self-belief will not happen overnight, but if you make a start, commit yourself and stay determined to see it through, there is every chance you will succeed.

Once you start to believe in yourself, your self-esteem will rise and you will gain more self-confidence. It is a continuous process and it never stops.

You won't always be confident or have a strong sense of self-belief, but you can reach a stage where you are more confident and self-assured most of the time. Working on your self-belief is the first step on the ladder to self-confidence, self-esteem and self-motivation. It will also help improve the quality of your life.

So, you have a choice to make. You can accept things as they are, or you can begin to explore your own potential and development. You owe it to yourself to take the risk and find out just how good you can be. Nobody ever improved without taking a risk. Small risk, small improvement – big risk, big improvement.

Just remember that whatever you choose to do with your life, you need to find the courage and self-belief to follow it through.

- Don't be put off from following your dreams, desires and aspirations.
- You will get a great deal of pleasure from doing something that other people said you couldn't do.
- Maximise your skills and talents.
- Challenge yourself to be the best that you can be.
- Challenge yourself to explore fully who you are and what you want out of life.
- Take the blinkers off and broaden your horizons.
- Have a belief in Your Self and work on your self-belief every day.

A final word on self-belief – think about all those who have inspired you. Think about people close to you that you look up to or admire. What is it about them that you like? What are the qualities that they have? What can you learn from them? Try to incorporate some of their ideals into yours.

YOU were successful before – you will be again!

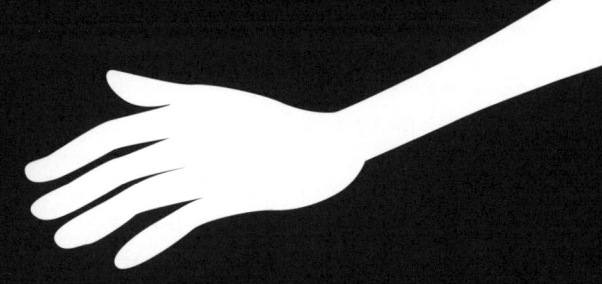

Chapter Thirteen

The Hysterical Self

This chapter is called The Hysterical Self for several reasons. First, laughter and laughing at ourselves is great therapy. Second, sometimes we take life too seriously and our problems too intensely, which is bad for our health.

We need to look at life and ourselves, and ask why we are rushing about 24/7. Is it any wonder that we have the highest incidence of heart failure, angina, high cholesterol levels, anxiety and stress in Europe? Somehow we need to slow down and take the time to laugh.

We all have the ability and capability to make someone laugh, but we don't do it often enough. We admire those people who appear to be naturally funny. But there's no reason why you shouldn't make it one of your aims in life to make someone smile or laugh each and every day. If everybody did this, what a different world it would be!

Your hysterical self is crying out to be released, so don't hold back. Laugh until your eyes water and your belly hurts! The effect on you and those around you will be infectious. Laughter helps us, both physically and psychologically. We feel better after a good laugh, and for a little while our worries and anxieties disappear. So we owe it to ourselves to nurture our 'hysterical self'.

Laughter is a universal right! It's free at the point of laughing.

So here are some funnies to get you in the mood:

> Q) What was the first thing your husband said to you when he woke this morning?
> A) He said: 'Where am I, Cathy?'
> Q) Why did that upset you?
> A) My name is Susan!

And another one:

> Prosecutor: What gear were you in when your vehicle collided with the other car?
> Defendant: Gucci sweats and Reeboks.

Laughter is strong medicine – even in a time of death, there can be laughter. It can also keep us young in heart and in mind. We admire those people who can produce a one-liner, a merry quip, or tell a joke, but you also have the ability to make people laugh.

Some of us are 'unconscious comedians', some have a quick wit, some can tell funny stories – but all of us have the power to make someone laugh. The tragedy in life is that as we get older, we seem somehow to lose our 'hysterical self' – usually during the dreaded teenage years.

It is often drummed into us to 'act your age'! So is it any wonder that a lot of the joys of life are taken away from us, and why so many people suffer from stress, anxiety, low self-esteem, lack of confidence – and a general unhappiness? We lose the joy of laughing. But a return to the simple joys of life will help you reconnect with your life and help put things in perspective.

- It is time to loosen that belt that has been strangling your love of life.
- It is time for you to laugh at the world and laugh at yourself.
- It is time to stop taking yourself too seriously.
- When was the last time that you really 'let yourself go'?
- Why don't you go and be outrageous?
- Forget about convention and society's urge for you to conform.
- Don't be worried about your age – do what makes you happy.

Age is just a number, and society dictates how that number should behave. But YOU have the chance to defy those restrictions. Don't let other people influence how you should behave, dress or act. Be who you want to be, laugh when you want to laugh. The next time you look at yourself in the mirror, why don't you have a good laugh at yourself? Remember, when you smile or laugh it adds to your face value.

Grandma Moses, of the USA

- did not start painting until she was 75 years of age

- she started painting because her arthritis was too painful to allow her to do her needlework anymore!

- by the time of her death – at the age of 101 – she had painted some 1600 pieces of work

Your Hysterical Self is bubbling away under the surface of your subconscious. By tapping into your funny side, you will release a volcano of pent-up joy and happiness. Inside every sad person there is a funny person waiting to come out. When was the last time you laughed so much that your stomach ached? When was the last time you made someone laugh?

Research has shown that by laughing we not only make ourselves happy, but we also make those around us feel good. It is no surprise that some hospitals are designed to be 'happy' places and staff encouraged to engage in humour with patients. It's not the first time that a request on hospital radio for the song 'The First Cut is the Deepest' has been requested for someone about to undergo surgery!

Your Hysterical Self is an important part of your armoury in the fight against boredom, staleness, conformity, anxiety, stress and even depression. If you can see the funny side of most things and laugh at yourself, then you're well on your way to having a happy, enriching and contented life. Sure, there will be obstacles in your way; there will be times when you just don't feel like being happy, or like laughing and seeing the funny side. There will also be life events that may rock you back on your heels. But your capacity to overcome all that life has to throw at you is helped by having a good, healthy Hysterical Self. Self-deprecating humour allows you to determine and control yourself in dealing with life's events. So don't shut yourself away from the simple joys of life – embrace them and laugh at them. Laugh at the absurdities of life.

The demands and pressures placed upon us are immense. We are all urged to be the same. Every day we are bombarded with adverts for this type of pill, that cream, these solutions – everything from stemming the tide of ageing to repairing hair loss.

Every day we are saturated with a myriad of alternative therapies that will cure all our ills. The latest therapy is called 'Whisper Therapy', used by couples who are experiencing difficulties in their relationship. It appears that couples have to 'look at themselves every 15 minutes, touch each other every few minutes and say words to each other about what they like about each other'.

However well-meaning they all are, all of these therapies – including CBT (Cognitive Behaviour Therapy) – are not a panacea for all of society's ills or problems. All offer something of value – some more than others.

The issue for people is to find out if they need one of the many therapies on offer. This book is intended for those who do not need an 'alternative therapist'. It is aimed at ordinary men and women who feel that perhaps life is passing them by, that they don't feel in control of what is going on in their lives. The advice is geared towards people who want to make a change to their lifestyle, who are fed up and feel they are in a rut. It aims to help them gain more belief in themselves, to rediscover the simple joys of life and to achieve and get more out of their life.

This book wants people to laugh a bit more. The emphasis on the Hysterical Self can be seen as a safety valve. How often has a good laugh lifted our spirits? Brought colour back to our cheeks?

Brought tears to our eyes? Laughter is the elixir of life! Without laughter, life would be very dull indeed so your Hysterical Self is your passport through life.

The old saying, 'Laugh and the world laughs with you – cry and you cry alone', has more than a grain of truth in it. When you let your Hysterical Self go, it's amazing the effect it has not only on you but on those around you.

- How often have you joined in laughing purely at the sound of someone else's laughing?
- We don't laugh often enough.
- We don't laugh loudly enough.

We are losing the art of laughter. You can have a virtual conversation with someone, a virtual relationship, virtual reality war, virtual reality dating, etc. But virtual reality laughter? We can make someone smile or even laugh using a text message or an e-mail, but there is no substitute for the sound of real laughing. So it is up to you to keep the flame of your Hysterical Self alive and burning brightly.

- Let it be a beacon for all to see and hear.
- It's up to you to work at seeing the funny side of life and to encourage others to do the same.
- Laughter is a serious business and it is no joke to find that a lot of life is without humour.
- All of us have it within us to bring a smile to someone's life.
- You have it within you to make someone happy – so why aren't you doing it?
- Why are you not spreading more happiness about?

When you have finished reading this chapter, why don't you go and make someone smile, make them happy and make their day – and yours? Have the courage to let your Hysterical Self shine through.

Can you make yourself laugh? Can you think of a funny punch line? Inside you is a funny person dying to come out. Being funny is a serious business for comedians, but for most of us it is a way of expression, comment and relief. It is vital that we laugh at ourselves and others, but we have become too sensitised and sanitised and are losing the art of being funny.

- Try and see the funny side of things.
- Laugh at the absurdities of everyday life.
- Promise to yourself that you will make someone smile every day.
- Making someone laugh or smile is one of the greatest gifts you can give.
- Cultivate your 'funny-bone', your funny side, your Hysterical Self.

- Don't be afraid to make a fool of yourself.
- The worst that can happen is that people will laugh at you. Good – now you know it works!

There are numerous books, films and shows, which have one purpose in mind – to make you laugh and help you escape from the drudgery of daily life. Your Hysterical Self comes into that category – it is designed to let you deal with life in a funny way.

You cannot escape humour – it's all around you. It is extremely difficult to imagine that there was any humour in the Nazi concentration camps – yet there were some surreal moments when the sound of laughter would reverberate round those dreary huts. Laughter can be a great safety valve in times of extreme danger.

But we won't end this cheerful chapter on a dark note. Laughter is the optimistic part of our lives. A comedian on stage may not be funny, but even that can be the source of humour after the event. There is laughter to be had in the most obscure situations and the most unusual of places and events, so don't let your Hysterical Self miss out on the fun. With all the current gloom and doom, it is even more important to find time to have a good laugh.

Here are a few thoughts to help us all to enjoy the simple things of life, and enrich the lives of others.

1) Make someone smile/laugh today and every day.

2) Look in the mirror and try NOT to laugh at yourself!
   (It can't be done.)

3) Laugh loudly – others will join in – it's infectious.

4) See the funny side of life – always.

5) SMILE – it adds to your face value.

6) A laugh a day keeps the pain at bay.

7) Take two drops of laughter every day.

8) Don't laugh at people – laugh with them.

9) Laughter is your safety valve. Use it or lose it!

10) Laughter is the medicine of life – don't get ill!

You may think that there's not a lot to be smiling about in these turbulent times – but that's where you're wrong. It is precisely in times like these that we turn to things that can help get us through. Laughter is one of those aspects of our lives that can ease the burden, however briefly, and take us away from the reality that we're currently experiencing. All need not be doom and gloom.

The richness of life is reflected in the amount of humour you have put into it and the amount of times you contributed to someone's happiness, which means you have a choice to make. You can wallow in the misery of your situation, or you can change the way you are approaching life. All you need to do is to smile a bit more, laugh a bit more and let yourself go. Life is to be enjoyed. Life is not a dress rehearsal – you have to make the most of it. Laugh and enjoy life. You owe it to yourself to make every day count, and be as happy as you can be.

Final word goes to that well-known philosopher and sage, Mr Marx. I mean Groucho – not Karl! He is quoted as saying: 'I, not events, have the power to make me happy or unhappy today. I can choose which it will be. Yesterday is dead; tomorrow hasn't arrived yet. I have just ONE day, Today, and I am going to be happy in it.' Sounds about right!

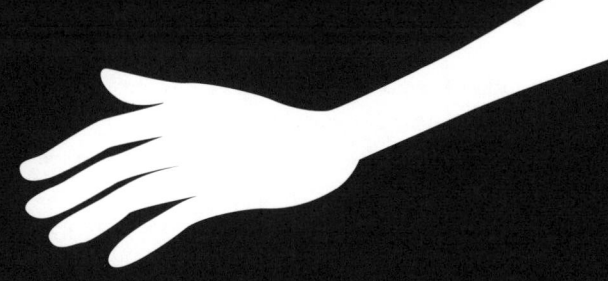

Chapter Fourteen

Take A Good Look At Your Self

How many times have you heard the above statement? And what exactly does it mean? Most parents will have said this to their children at one time or another, usually in a derogatory manner or as a put-down.

But there is a more positive way that we can look at the statement. If you can stand back and 'take a good look at yourself', who do you see when you look at your reflection in the mirror? By 'taking a good look at yourself', you will begin to self-analyse who and what you are.

Taking time to reflect on your life and where it is going is no bad thing. Some people use the quiet solitude of a visit to a church, a walk along a beach, a jog, or just simply enjoy the peace and quiet of an evening. The time to reflect and to have a good look at ourselves will help us to define who we are and to keep things in perspective.

By taking the time to stop and think, we can gather our thoughts and plan for the next day, week, month or year ahead. We can either keep on the course we are already on or set sail for another destination altogether. We can also review our progress and how far we have come in our journey through life.

There is an old saying that we improve our lives by experience. This is not exactly accurate. We only really improve when we reflect on the experience. You do not need to spend an enormous amount of time reflecting.

Subconsciously many of us do it on a daily basis, and sometimes throughout the day. What we don't do is to consciously make time available – to review, to evaluate and to plan ahead.

Have a good look at yourself. Maybe you have clung on to things for too long. Have you had a good look at the clothes you wear? Have you convinced yourself that your appearance doesn't matter and that nobody notices or cares? Do you care? Have you convinced yourself of that old chestnut that 'it's not the clothes I wear, but who is inside them that matters'?

Is your life in such a condition that it is verging on the robotic? Do you feel trapped? Would you like to change part of your life? Believe it or not, the answer begins inside your head. Take a blank piece of paper and write down all those things that are good in your life. Once you have done that, write down those aspects of your life that you would like to change. Once that has been completed, leave the lists alone and take some time out to reflect on them. When you are ready to return, go to the list of changes that you want to make.

Select one aspect from the list that you really want to work on immediately.

- Take a fresh, blank page and write in large letters the issue or goal that you want to change or pursue.
- Now study that carefully and underneath write down all the things you think will need to happen for you to achieve that change.
- Remember small steps are vitally important.
- Once you have decided what you want to change and how you are going to do it, the next part is just that – go and do it!

Once you have done the first item on your list, tick it off. You will immediately feel a bit more self-confident. Nothing breeds success like success. Small successes will encourage you to continue and ultimately lead to bigger successes. There is something prophetic when people say 'Rome wasn't built in a day'. To change your outlook on life will take more than one day.

> Remember Bethany Hamilton? She was the 13-year-old surfer who was destined to become a world champion until she was attacked by a 14ft shark one day. She lost her arm but was determined to surf again. After only six weeks, she was back in the water, and that same year she finished fourth in a major surfing competition!

We all recall the children's fairy-tale, Snow White, when the Evil Queen looks into the mirror and asks, 'Mirror, mirror on the wall, who is the fairest of them all?' Have you looked in the mirror? Are you the fairest of them all today? Mirrors don't lie – what you see is what you see, but the mirror can't show what is inside us. What it shows is only the physical side of us – it can't show our mental side. The main stumbling block to your progress is staring right back at you. If you can overcome YOU on a daily basis, then you have every chance of succeeding in the changes you want to make to your life.

Many people are too self-conscious about looking at themselves in a mirror. Although most of us are not in the Brad Pitt or Angelina Jolie mode, we all have a beauty that is unique to us.

- Celebrate your uniqueness and your individuality.
- Remember there is nobody quite like you – you are unique.
- You are valued as person in your own right.
- Do not let people put you off your dreams or aspirations.
- You owe it to yourself to be who you want to be.
- You deserve whatever success will come your way.

Start by taking 20 seconds to look at yourself in a mirror, just to remind yourself of just how good you are. Go on, you know you can do it. Then you can decide what you are going to do to overcome 'YOU'. This is the first big hurdle for you to overcome. Stand back for a moment and mentally remind yourself, again and again, just how good you are. If you keep on saying it, you will come to believe it.

This constant repeating of a positive message will help you overcome those negative thoughts that you have. All too often we allow ourselves to be influenced by negative thinking. It seems easier to hold a negative thought than a positive one. So, every time a negative thought comes into your head, quickly press the remote control in your head to a positive channel. Mental thinking is just like watching TV. When a programme comes on that you don't like or feel uncomfortable with (negative thinking), you can change the programme to something more relaxing (positive thinking).

Taking a good look at yourself and reflecting on who you are, what you are and where you want to go, is a necessary part of your ongoing development as a person. You will change physically, mentally and biologically as you get older. Some of these changes can be hard to accept, but if you can keep a healthy mind-set you will be able to cope with them better. Just because our age increases does not mean that our ambitions or desires should decrease, or that we should stop doing things we did when we were younger. The onset of age does not preclude us from achieving great things, because age is no barrier to achievement.

Take a good look at yourself and make a conscious decision to change. Make a commitment to yourself to keep chasing your rainbow. Be determined that whatever your goals in life, you will continue to keep going no matter what lies ahead. Start the process now – firmly believe that you can... and you will! If you don't believe in yourself, who will? If you don't believe in you can – you won't. Life is a battle of 'WILLS' – it's between I will and I will not.

The dark fears of negativity are sometimes hard to overcome, but not impossible. You can start to overcome them when you look at Your Self and make that conscious decision to change. Nothing is static forever – all things change. The trick is to take control and direct the change in a way that benefits you. Prepare yourself for that change. Alter your current mind-set and change the look you have in the mirror to a new you!

Your life is like a fashion show, with many changes taking place and covering all the seasons. All you have to do is to respond to the seasonal changes and walk confidently down the catwalk of life. All of us have the mental strength within us to alter the way we think and behave.

- Unlock the real you by realising the potential you have to achieve those things that you have always dreamt of.
- Break down the barriers of restraint.
- Smash the mirror (not literally) of negativity and let yourself start with a new beginning.

- Constantly remind yourself how much you're a valued member of society with so much to contribute.
- Decide now what you want to change.
- Choose what 'road' you want to travel on. Is it the road to mediocrity? Or the road to success, which has many wrong turns, dead-ends and one way streets?

To change direction you need to be sure which direction you want to go in then take the first tentative steps. Those changes do not need to be big, dramatic statements, just small but significant stepping stones. These stepping stones will give you the necessary encouragement to carry on.

Don't be afraid to look into that mirror of your life. Sometimes we have to face some harsh realities – unemployment, death, moving house, relationship breakdown. The stress and anxiety of dealing with these issues can make things very difficult for us. They can shake us to the very core of our being. But it is how we respond and react to them that is the issue.

No matter what life throws at us, it is vital that we do not succumb to bitterness and regret. Your life is important to you and you owe it to yourself to make the most of what you have. This does not mean that you have to abandon your responsibilities or commitments, but it does mean that you have to try twice as hard to keep the flame of self-fulfillment burning and not allow it to flicker and die in the wind.

- Keep a positive frame of mind – no matter how tough things get.
- Never give up on your dreams and ambitions.
- Search for new ways to improve your life.
- You owe it to yourself – nobody else – to do the things that you want to do.

All too often the skills and talents that so many people have are left behind in a sea of 'if only…'. Turn that 'if only' into 'will do'. You can't wait for the perfect conditions to appear before you make a change – it will never happen. You have to make things happen for yourself. There is no such thing as luck, only circumstances. You have to create the right circumstances for yourself. It's time to make a start so:

Take a good look at Your Self!

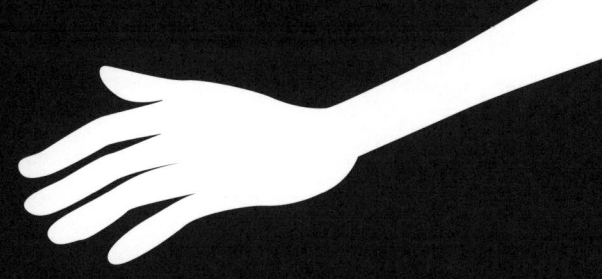

Chapter Fifteen

The Final Self

At last... The final chapter in the book!

The Final Self is, of course, all about you. By now you should know who you are. Throughout the book, I have asked you not to deny your right to be who you are. Accept yourself, believe in yourself, and believe in what you want to get out of life.

I have challenged you to make a start by doing something that pleases you, and you alone. That means you have to stop trying to please other people all the time and to be a bit more SELFISH! You need to find some time for your Quiet Self. No matter how busy you are – no matter the pressures you may be under – you need to find time for some peace and quiet. Those moments of reflection allow you to gather your thoughts and prepare you to enjoy what life has to offer. Now is the time to turn those dreams, desires and aspirations into reality.

The Final Self is all about what you want out of life and what you're prepared to do about it.

- Start by changing your 'old' outlook and decide you want much more out of life.
- Begin to see the world in an entirely different light.
- Think about all the good things in your life and how much more you want to get out of it.
- You owe it to yourself to keep on learning about and developing your Self.
- Life is one big learning trip!
- Never stop challenging, stretching, demanding and pushing yourself.

Sadly, too many people give up on themselves because it gets too hard, or they allow 'obstacles' to get in their way. This means they give up on their dreams and aspirations.

They have probably listened to the wrong people for too long. They have allowed the voices of negative people – saying 'you're too young, too old, not big enough, too tall, not good enough, strong enough,' etc – to creep into their mind-set and confirm their own private fears.

This final chapter is telling you to say, 'Enough is Enough!' You will no longer listen to what negative people have to say. Instead, you will hear the positive voice within you. It is time to shake off those chains that have bound you to a life of underachievement, mediocrity, low self-esteem, low self-confidence, low self-worth and, ultimately, sadness.

Your Final Self will not allow you to accept things just because they have always been that way. You know now who You are! In fact, you know Your Self better than anybody else on this earth.

So you can change the way you feel and the way you see yourself.

With a change in attitude comes a change in commitment. I'm asking you to commit yourself to making that change – NOW! Don't be afraid – you will be amazed at what you can accomplish, once you have accepted your Final Self, and you start to make demands of yourself.

- Don't swim in the pool of self-pity and 'if only'; jump into the water of life.
- Embrace change.
- Give yourself permission to be who you are and what you want to be.
- Allow time and space for YOU.
- Be Selfish, and don't apologise for it.
- Seek out new adventures, new routes and new challenges.
- Push yourself to achieve and believe.
- Don't be like so many who give up at the first hurdle, or at the first sign of disappointment or setback – stay with it.
- Demand the right to be who YOU want to be.
- Have confidence in yourself and start to believe you CAN, instead of you can't.
- If you don't feel confident, then ACT confident – and confidence will eventually be yours.
- Your Final Self is waiting for you to begin.

The Final Self is the last journey in the voyage of self-discovery. Once you have completed your journey of self-discovery, the Final Self will lead you on the road to being more self-confident, self-assured and happy within yourself.

Not everyone can reach the summit of Mount Everest, but all of us can enjoy the journey of aiming for the top, admiring the scenery, marvelling at the steps we take along the way, appreciating what life has to offer and enjoying every day that we live. Remember it's not the cards of life that you are dealt that count – but how you play them.

What did Inspector Dreyfus in the Pink Panther films, say? 'Every day and every way, I get a little better.' Make small adjustments to your life and watch them make an impact. Nothing stands still. Everything changes – including you.

The Final Self is an amalgam of all the 'selfs' in this book. It is the culmination of all that is required for you to be who you want to be. The Final Self is the final decider as to whether or not you go forward in life with renewed vigour, commitment and determination to change, or whether you remain static.

Don't just accept things as they are. Don't allow those dark forces of negativity to take hold and stop you from doing what you want to do.

Every day is a constant battle of wills between the forces of negativity and positivity. So learn to win those daily battles. Change your negative mind-set into a positive one. They say that mirrors don't lie – what you see is reflected in who and what you are.

The Final Self will start you on a journey that you have never experienced before. It will open up new horizons for you, new opportunities. It will enable you to explore further who you are and what you are capable of. The Final Self will tap into those hidden resources, abilities and desires that lie beneath the surface of your inner self. This will lead to an increase in your self-belief and to a more fulfilling lifestyle. In addition, you will increase your self-confidence and have a greater determination and commitment to succeed.

You will be amazed at the untapped abilities, skills and talents that you always had but were afraid either to show or work at. Don't be one of those people who have had the talent, ability or skill, but never let it grow. Why do so few people realise their ambitions? What has happened to those who harboured dreams, hopes and desires? Who put their flame of hope out?

Have you reached the top of your personal Everest? If not, why not? And what are you going to do about it? Not everyone can be a top sportsperson, author or entrepreneur, but we can all improve on what we have and maximise our talents, abilities and skills. We can improve the quality of our lives even in a small way, by learning new skills, taking a course at college, or joining an exercise class. Whatever it takes to improve the quality of our lives, we should do it.

Trust your Final Self to lead you in a new and invigorating direction. You have nothing to lose but your mediocrity. Put some meaning back into your life. Whenever you decide to do something, you immediately make a change forever. You can never go back. You can only go forward – with hope, confidence and an unyielding self-belief. Only you can make a difference to your life – others and circumstances can help but, in the final analysis, it is what you do that will ultimately count.

Have faith in your Final Self. Be a positive force for change. The satisfaction that you will get will exceed your expectations and wildest dreams. It is time to turn those dreams into reality. Turn your 'I can't' into 'I CAN!'

Set yourself on a new course of self-discovery and self-achievement. If life is a risk, just how much of a risk are you prepared to take? If life is worth living, what are you living for? If life is a challenge, what is your challenge? If life has a purpose, what is your purpose? If everything changes, why can't you?

With so many questions to be answered, it is easy to get overawed by the task ahead. But the fundamental premise is that of enjoyment. There is not much point in making any changes to your life if it is not enriched by laughter, enjoyment and fun. All too often these three ingredients are missing. It's as if they are an add-on to what we do, instead of becoming the cornerstone of our existence.

Life can be very hard and some of the setbacks we experience can leave us bereft of any form of levity. But somehow we have to overcome them, stay focused and true to ourselves, and remember that laughter is a vital ingredient in our fight for survival and progress. Even in the darkest of times we need our sense of humour. Never be afraid to laugh and enjoy life to the full. Be true to Your Self. Look after Your Self.

The Final Self will decide which path you take. The Final Self will decide just how much determination and commitment you have to make the necessary changes that will affect your life. All through this book you have been set challenges and offered different ways of looking at yourself. All that is asked of you is to take the time to reflect on your life and, if you're not totally happy or satisfied, then do something about it.

Nobody will come, tap you on the shoulder and give you a better life. You have to get up, go out and make it happen. Whatever dreams you once had for yourself may have diminished or faded over the years. But that shouldn't stop you from having new dreams, goals or aspirations. We are only restricted in what we can achieve by the mental barriers and boundaries that we have allowed into our mind-set. Get rid of those words that end in 'n't' like 'Can't' or 'Won't'. Replace them with 'I Can' and 'I Will'.

One of the many words in the dictionary is 'doubt' – leave it there! Dismiss the doubters from your mind – they have nothing positive to say or to contribute. Avoid those who say to you that this or that can't be achieved, and that you can't make those changes.

- Stretch yourself to the fullest.
- Exploit your skills and talents.
- Be Selfish – you owe it to yourself.
- It's your life, nobody else's and you have to make the most of what you have.
- You have a right to be happy.
- You have a right to explore how far you can go and what you can be.
- You have the right to be YOU.
- You have a right to know you.

The search for the Real You is over. Now that you know who you are and what you want, get out there and grab life with both hands. It's just CSP!